Praise for Across the Distance

"Christina Kemp has composed a remarkable book. Her second-person messages to her parents, her brother, friend, and lovers delve deeply into the essence of relationships with a voice that ranges from analytical to poetic. The missives are as unique as the recipients, yet threads of love, pain, and longing bind the essays together. Readers will find resonances of their own loves and losses in these pages, and the magic and music of her words will echo in their hearts."

—Seán Dwyer, author of *A Quest for Tears: Surviving Traumatic Brain Injury*

"The depth of Kemp's well-earned psychological insights make it so deeply satisfying to inhabit her reflections. *Across the Distance* is honest, wrenchingly painful in its clarity, and rich in its expression of the simultaneity of the emotional life. The style of writing is also fascinating. Kemp presents an observing or spectating commentary in the indented segments, as though the therapeutic gaze is offered afterwards. A truly remarkable and profound expression. Kemp is a gifted writer and healer, and her memoir is an inspiring prospect for anyone who reads it. *Across the Distance* is an invitation to explore the complexity and nuance of our most sensitive and formative relationships and the courage to find access to the intelligence of our own suffering."

—Claire Lebeau, Ph.D., Associate Professor, Psychologist

"*Across the Distance* reads like a series of love letters to the self: poignant, touching, and compelling in what is offered in between the lines, as much as in the written word. It works within the reader as a slow blossoming that happens when one begins to understand the whispers of the soul.

Depth psychology—soul-centered psychology—focuses on the study of the unconscious: what lies beneath the surface of things in the invisible world. In this book, Kemp gives voice to what is often unspoken, but deeply felt in everyday life. Through a series of beautifully nuanced and archetypal motifs and vignettes, the reader is tenderly directed toward the center of herself and invited to explore the inner landscapes of love and loss in order make space for the unimaginable beauty of what is already here."

—Bonnie Bright, Ph.D., Founder of Depth Insights,
Depth Psychology Alliance, and the Institute for
Soul-Centered Psychology and Coaching

Across the Distance

Reflections on Loving

and

Where We Did & Did Not Find Each Other

Christina A. Kemp

Across the Distance

Reflections on Loving
and
Where We Did & Did Not Find Each Other

Christina A. Kemp

Sidekick Press
Bellingham, Washington

This memoir represents the author's recollection of her past. These true stories are faithfully composed based on memory, photographs, diary entries, and other supporting documents. Some names, places, and other identifying details have been changed to protect the privacy of those represented. Conversations between individuals are meant to reflect the essence, meaning, and spirit of the events described.

Published 2022
Printed in the United States of America
ISBN: 978-1-7365358-8-2
LCCN: 2021921140

Sidekick Press
2950 Newmarket Street, Suite 101-329
Bellingham, Washington 98226
sidekickpress.com

Christina A. Kemp, 1985-

Across the Distance: Reflections on Loving and Where We Did & Did Not Find Each Other

Cover concept and image by Christina A. Kemp
Cover design by Andrea Gabriel

For my dad

Contents

Letter to the Reader

In these pages lay stories of trying to come together amid many ways we are often separate, and apart.

Perhaps you will glimpse where metaphor exists amid what is also tangible and concrete—and perceive a dance that unfolds between interiority and the outer circumstances of narrative. Somewhere between our personal experiences and the events through which we unfold flow truths we may never fully grasp— but in trying to relay what has happened in our lives, and discern what is subjective, numinous, ineffable, and partial or unknown, we experience greater depth and richness.

Loving is fraught within the terrain of complexity. Just when we think we understand what is simple and clear, we must be willing to acknowledge what is unfinished or obscure. Absolution drags us away from tolerating the mystery between moments we have woven into stories of meaning . . .

My hope is that through standing more thoughtfully and openly toward our stories, we may more readily sense the many layers within ourselves and between us all. Perhaps then we may eventually hold ourselves and each other for more of what we really are.

This book may be read in any order—through a sequential whole, or one piece at a time.

~ Christina

Photo by John Kemp

Acknowledgments

To my eighth-grade biology teacher, Ms. Conner, who handed me my first journal. Karyn Frazier, the first voice to name that I could write—your words were a granule I held to and built from. To the other voices who echoed support for my writing in its early years—Jeanette Wilde, Hilary Wilson, Christina Rohlik, and Evan Hernandez, I thank you.

To Tricia Hagen, Elizabeth Barton, Liza Ziliak, and Debbie Ritter—yours were the great presences of support I needed to motion through waves of healing. I hold you each in an eternal place. To Laurie Belliveau, for generously holding me through a season of hardship. To Margaret Shepherd, Tim and Michelle Cayford, and Judith Allison—I am not a home without your enduring love in my life. And Helen Heaslip, you have impacted my embodied life for the better.

To my brother, Christopher, who has always encouraged my accomplishments with joy. To my Grandma Gayle, for supporting me through many seasons of becoming.

To Cami Ostman, who burgeoned a communal holding for this writing to reveal, transform, and revise itself. To my critique group, Mary Lou Haberman, Dana Tye Rally, and Ingrid Roeske

Goode, for creating a warm place during the sensitive months of this book's formation: you relayed an essence of ongoing encouragement and thoughtful reflection that cannot be spoken. And Cheryl Nelson, your wisdom perceived the exact dose of subtlety and insight this book needed in its final phase of birthing.

To my publisher, Lisa Dailey, at Sidekick Press, for seeing within these pages something worthy of being placed in the world. I knew I could place what is sacred in your hands. And to my editor, Dana Tye Rally, whose sensitivity and intelligence encourages what is written to come together in the most authentic and readable way possible.

And finally, to my mom and dad: you brought me into a divine mystery, full of loss and unutterable love, with hope, in the best way you knew how. *Thank you.*

Photo by Shaun Swalley

Currents

— Tommy —

I was drawn to click the mouse by something more powerful than my reluctance. I sighed past the resistance, rolling my eyes, uncomfortably filling out the profile, crying, murmuring *fuck this* under my breath, over and over. On an early April night, clarity beneath thought—intuition—propelled me there, simple and clear.

I've felt clarity that way before. Pulling me toward what will continue my lesson in becoming, never certain of what the outcome will be—

and following, just the same.

We have pieces of ourselves, scab-like and ill-fitting, that need to soften and shed if we are to continue deepening into who we really are.

The process, never ceasing, is always ongoing, though it can still be deterred.

I remember this as I ask through the years which aspects of myself have retained a sense of life, and which have perhaps outgrown their usefulness. As I reflect in each new season on whether the core of who I am is what I continue living into. Trying to motion from a soulful place that is never removed—but can still be forgotten.

I know we long to move past wounding we have accrued—

where we have taken on the inheritances of what remains untransformed and passed on from the lives of others, and interspersed those neglected terrains within our own becoming.

What is unhealed interweaves into the sense of ourselves—muddying a still pool of water, meant to be so clear.

Making us forget who we really are—

and yet drawing us together, all the same.

Perhaps we find our way to each other so that we can remember.

Re-member.

There was a flood of men coming at me, with their images and introductory prompts through the screen. I rubbed my eyes, tired, not wanting to be there, but acknowledging in some trickling thirst, I had shown up just the same. I tried to engage someone, reluctantly, but it was too dry from the outset. I discontinued, the genuine interest I needed lacking.

Part of me didn't want to follow the instinct that prompted me to continue—but I knew, without knowing why, that I was supposed to. Venturing within the contradiction, seeking to discover more clearly the opposing ends, I continued to scroll, partaking in the motions, not really knowing what this was going to be about. Trusting the silent opening within the paradox, that held some gravitational draw.

The intuition that called with its level of clarity from that night—
felt like tuning into an invitation from the clear voice of God.

It wasn't long before I saw you. Your face, and simple, relaxed
smile, held some resonance of what had drawn me. And your natural comfort with yourself, the humble authenticity of few and
simple words lacking egoism and awkwardness—feelings of force
ceasing to perfuse their way in through the awkward and mechan-
ical medium. You were the "few years older" guy crush I'd always
had, but that never amounted to much during my younger years.
Shaggy hair, easy smile. Tall and thin. Warm beneath a hooded
sweatshirt. Easygoing and comfortable in your own skin.

The inbox kept filling. Messages I ignored.

I simply just waited, for you.

As I sat on the edge of the seat of hopeful curiosity and bor-
dering disappointment—a day or two later, not having yet heard
from you.

Turned out there was a delay in the system's overlay, and you had
been waiting for a response, just the same.

We spent that first weekend feeling each other out—writing
letters and taking calls, feeling so quickly and suddenly the alignment between us. My jaw dropping open, as I read not only the
fluid beauty of your written words, but so too your familiarity
with Jung, Campbell, psychological studies, healers, and the like.
Raised Christian, but not so much anymore—

yes, yes, deeply spiritual.

Your love of music—the ground of your identity—and that
graceful, generous interest you imparted toward my own interests
in teaching, writing, dancing . . .

Genuine and thoughtful engagement.

You signed a letter that weekend "Yours."

And wanting to discover more, I kept following the opening for what it was.

Unknown.

Three weeks later, I drove down the rainy, black highway toward Portland, listening to the *Great Expectations* film score by Patrick Doyle. Outside, I felt the darkness and rain as it scattered repeatedly, pitter-patting against my windshield, which encased the warmth of my vehicle. An old, jazzy rhythm splashed with the memories of the days we had just been together, as I made my way toward that undiscovered city—and again, toward you. Two days before, you had come to Seattle for our first meeting, and with less than a day gone by, we were once again making our way toward each other—unable to wait another day.

I can still remember the trepidation I felt when I first beheld your presence that first weekend in Seattle. I was hovering near the *Psychology* section on the second floor of The Elliot Bay Book Company, waiting for you to arrive, when I caught a glimpse of you on the ground floor below. You entered the building and began to exchange words with an old friend who you'd run into on your way toward the stairs. My stomach fluttered slightly,

 with a subtle anticipation,

 and then small, settled dropping—

 the kind that came from seeing: you weren't exactly what

 I'd expected.

Even from far away, atop those second-story floorboards . . .

When you climbed the stairs and we were finally face-to-face, I was still holding the previous weeks' anticipations, and soon found myself trying to retain those loose but forming structures so that they would remain in the forefront of my mind—as you stood over me, tall, in a dark coat, and I felt a subtle-but-clear cautiousness in my concern,

as I looked in your eyes,

and saw a glimpse of potential unhinging.

We'd spent hours every day during the previous weeks getting to know each other—writing, talking—and I had not detected any hints of concern. That developing base between us kept me open to you, as I sat before you in suspended curiosity and we ate sandwiches together in a crowded restaurant amid the cluttering of voices and noise.

We all have specks of quirkiness, pockets of psychic disease—and while the degrees of separation are hardly inconsequential, I was determined to acknowledge the full collaging of who you were. Knowing how my subtle myopia had propelled me toward eye-opening unfoldings about my own undigested wounds in the past . . .

Even amid the noise, a connection remained resonate between us, of what echoes beneath the limitations of our surface worlds, that reminded me also—

it is more than our wounds that draws us together.

In that first weekend, as we passed the hours together, I walked beside you into the discovery of a deep sense of closeness and ease in being. Responses, of "Me too!" were followed quickly by reverberations of "Oh, and that's where we differ . . ." as we discovered where we were both different and the same. Your insights into emotional and psychological processing and capacity for interdisciplinary thought made me feel better understood than the glazed-over and confused eyes I was used to seeing reflected back to me from the minds of other men. You gestured genuinely to *see* what others only skimmed the surface of in the interweaving complexities and sensitivities that are my own soul. And I met you there, in the binding turmoil and desires that were your own, as I looked into your face next to mine, and moved a coarse, brown strand of hair away from the green shadows of your eyes with the soft tip of my fingers. And the arousal I felt, that was beyond words, that first moment in the dark woodiness of an up-stairs pub, when your incredibly soft lips touched mine and you paused—and then caressed the inside of my mouth with the yin-like force of your tongue.

You placed your hand softly upon my face—and I was drawn into more of you. Through the opening of feeling between us, something began erupting within me: a steady and lingering sort of passion I had not fully felt before.

I loved kissing you, ever since.

And so, as I parked my deep blue Jeep beneath the trees of your small apartment in Portland after arriving that late rainy evening, I approached the dim lit doors of the musty, turn-of-the-century building where you lived, and neither of us could wait to be to-gether again.

I wrapped my arms around the tall thin of your waist, and turned my cheek upon your chest, smelling your sweet, vanilla-laced scent lingering upon the soft of your shirt as you held me back, and softly but happily said, "Hi."

"I bought us dinner. It's waiting inside. Do you want a bath?"

Your thoughtful gestures, from offering to draw the water, to the dinner and music you prepared, all amid the soft-lit hue of your small studio apartment minimally and tastefully decorated, was such an attractive and welcome kindness, and relief. As I remembered indif-ference, and lackadaisical approaches, that I had been met with by other men.

And when you didn't even attempt to kiss me again, for hours, it only furthered my own feeling of being drawn toward you.

When our mouths finally did meet, we flowed in the gentle current carrying us toward more.

Making love to you was a wave of ease—synchronous, flowing, and intimate. We looked into each other's eyes, opening something gentle between us and comforting beneath the touch of our hands. The absence of a distanced, fog-like barrier of removal, so often present in supposedly intimate places, was replaced by absorption and presence. We just simply looked, and kissed, and moved together, as if we had been looking and kissing and moving from a time primordial.

I think we'd known each other and had been in loving entrapments across lifetimes.

The way that we so easily fit together, and could motion and move—fingers entwining in your sheets—

and later, down the cold chill of city sidewalks, as we walked lovingly, embraced with softness and contentment.

Your protectiveness that emerged, strongly, as you squeezed my hand while we crossed busy streets—

and the way I would soon sense the darkness I could so easily bind to within you, in the psychic undercurrents of our joint entrapments of pain.

Sometimes what we feel with someone echoes something more ancient than what is tangible along the waves of time.

As the weeks passed, each of us traveled to see the other as often as we could, and I watched the leaves of trees flurry past train windows as wheels sped down the tracks to take me back toward you.

We stayed together in your apartment when I went south, and in the quaint and comfortable homes of B&Bs by the water when you came north. Peaceful and settled—we experienced some unnamable harmony in being able to engage the artistries of our minds and emotional worlds with affinity and understanding. And then after a slow talk in the rising morning rays, we would settle back once again, into a gently held rhythm and pace of just being.

Hands held, quietly sitting on a back porch.

Coffee and tea, your guitar, by the water.

Seagulls flew overhead, and I snapped a picture of you facing the ocean under the sun.

You and I were never ignited in the frenzy and temporary passions that lift us farther off the ground more than they settle us down upon it.

Our being together flowed with a quiet kind of ease that felt settled and close.

Like we were the oldest of friends.

We developed that friendship alongside the attraction we explored, as we walked throughout Japanese gardens, and ventured into each other's pasts. Uncovering the wounds that lay there, our places of messiness were offered before each other—and they became seen, and held caringly, as we returned home, to descend into the warm waters of a bath, and we leaned into each other's arms, our bodies wrapped around one another.

Peaceful, quiet moments spread around the room—

and sunlight moved across tile floors and painted walls.

Your head with wet hair was leaning into my cheek. And we had silent presence, *together*.

"I feel something for you, but I'm not going to say it yet," you said one night, one month in, after the lapping waters of the tub had been released, and you were facing away from me in the kitchen.

I smiled, knowing I felt the same.

Very early, in our time together side by side, brief moments began to arise—meteoric, quickly passing but unignorable—that told me there was something within the complexity of who you were that could reflect a familiar harmful current of my past.

A defensiveness that seemed disproportionate to what was being said; a responsiveness that felt compensatory for something unnamed beneath the surface.

It was the kind of egoic fragility that echoed instability; something that endures beyond mere moments of human messiness.

The reminders of where I came from did little to evoke feelings of comfort, and yet they informed my capacity—a toleration and slowed breathing amidst the defensive rise.

And also, my engagement.

I was familiar with the sensations that laced me inside, those which accompany sweeping extremes of responses from others that so often stem from a fixed and embedded wounding that will not nudge.

"I expect some goddamned respect." The comment seemed to appear out of nowhere. You glared into a space I could not see and breathed heavily, one afternoon outside the walls of a café, on the patio where I had offered you a different point of view.

I didn't leave, even when I saw what began to emerge. More than the fear of the rising tides, I felt I needed to discover *how far to tread* in order to know clearly whether these waters would become those in which I could not again submerge . . .

I watched the moments as they unfolded, and felt them through, holding their resonances closely, as I reflected—

and discerned the accumulating fragments of the frame.

And then, I slowly paced myself, through fearful tremors that echoed howling sounds of past and present inside an obscure terrain, as I tried to decipher what was mine—

the past reworking within the present,

what in me willingly wanted to reengage a slippery, downhill tumble toward areas of my own unclaimed psyche,

fearful interpretations that could be misunderstood and projected—

and what was yours.

Facts can be detailed inside the mind, but if what begins forming is the loose structure of a story we know to be true, but which remains *unfelt as truth*, the script will be of little use next to gravity that pulls us from deep inside. The weight that exists within the confines of feeling must find its way to the half-light truth of our minds if we are to ever *move* the constellating life within us, meaningfully.

I needed to bridge the discord within me, to be *whole* as I sensed my way through the semblance of a story I still wondered could possibly lead to a different ending.

We can spend a lot of time looking at pictures, instead of looking into the eyes of the person before us.

I began to wonder: *Is this what I do with you?*

I looked far away, and watched you—the way you stood in thought, the way you held yourself, the cigarette in your hand. I read your words, and wondered—*did they hold such wisdom?*

There were times when I felt this was the case.

But in your movements, I began to wonder whether you knew how to placate. You were so intelligent and adaptable—I watched the way you interacted with a server at the bar, the way you discussed the poetry of what you loved, the *music*. And, too, conversations between you and your brother. The waitress at our table. Full of kindness, lovingness, and ease. But then behind closed doors, the way you would speak of these interactions as the engagements which drained, and took you from "the only two things you truly cared about in life"—*love and music.*

I heard the utterances of contempt and blame as you spoke about the way you "needed" to take care of validating other people's feelings—and the way this kept you from *being fully and truly yourself.*

"Everyone," you said, when I asked who for?

Everyone.

Was I to find myself in the box of exclusion, in the shade that kept you from your "true light"?

. . . or was I part of the love, that thing that you said you lived for, deep inside?

The names of friends, who was and wasn't, would change and merge: sliding from one category and then back out, as if the placement depended on the mood or the circumstantial breeze. I wasn't naïve enough to consider myself exempt from this sliding, changing view from which you saw others and the world. *Was it a bad day?* A fleeting moment of vented frustration and anger?

. . . or was it something else within you, some more enduring instability, that you wished to hide.

The sweetness I knew in you left abruptly, the night you threw the phone that carried my enlivened face within the frame. *Slamming* me shut—throwing me aside in one, violent sweep.

And the way I could no longer find my way past the shield you had forged between us.

I recognized that impenetrability.

And kept wondering where you went that night.

Today, I still go back, to the places we've been. I walk along Ballard Avenue, and stop, pausing, in the frame of the doorway where we once stood together. Or the French bakery, the first morning I felt the skin of the back of your fingers softly touch mine: knuckles, and soft. We sat at a small corner table, reading. Outside, you stood in the cold. I was wrapped in the largeness of your black coat; you smoked, and we spoke of Montana.

I pass where we walked throughout a garden. We were in *The Garden*, weren't we? We spoke of so much sameness, and I cried out with laughter as water came falling in fat sprinkling drops to dampen the enveloping green. The moments of simple joy, and comfort in understanding, we found together.

I'm sitting on the edge of what's man-made, facing the Sound. Water laps and caresses the blocked cement below me, and I listen. The waves beat and spray, white-capped further on in the distance, and I find myself wondering: *How can such peace exist alongside such danger?* The waves offshore are tousled and turning, and though glimmering specks of sunlight dapple and play upon the surface, there is what I know to be that deep, darkened pull of the undercurrents beneath.

Wasn't this my experience of you? Motioning, in harmony, with you by my side, whether near or far apart—but soon contacting the turmoil that existed beside that wonderful but brief breeze of peace we found ourselves upon? Wandering deeper into togetherness, only to find tender moments of a growing love would not be sustained alongside those unknown waters: the violence and rage that brewed. *Could not* be sustained . . .

Still, I wanted you with me.

We slowly began to carve a space *between* the prior paths in our lives—and discovered where differences between what we had known before might exist between us as we hoped to be brought into a new *enough* way of being.

Not everything is a clear overlap with the past. And not all themes can be drawn and connected through time to fit one singular description or category.

Your *differences*, the ones I began seeing in you, were significant for me—

the way you could actually *name* with some awareness, your demons. When you said, "I know I have a problem with this. I'm working on it, to be better."

Together, we started to carve that path. It gave me such hope—the way we recognized, acknowledged, and tried.

Perhaps that's what made what came after so painful. The knowledge that what was being lost was not rooted only in a *dream* of possibility—

but in the actual tangibility of what we had begun to experience, together.

Because for that brief moment in time, we listened to each other with openness, willingness, and friendship, and did not avoid the painful terrain that rarely wants to be to be named—

"I didn't realize I scared you. I'm sorry."

Yes, you did . . .

The sensation of slight pricking slowly started stemming throughout my reawakening nerves, and began moving toward the limbs of my remembrances, further reactivating what can never be truly forgotten.

I steadied myself outwardly, became quiet and still, while inwardly, I knew—and grew nauseous at the recognition . . .

Despite the repairs, I began to ask an old familiar question:

What do I have to hold back within myself for the sake of not upsetting something further?

The weight of the love and friendship was more than I had encountered in another before who had shared similar patterns of behavior.

That love and friendship was important to me.

I held my hand out toward you, again, as I felt you slipping away—"We're on the same team."

You were reluctant—

but still, you came with me . . .

I began having heartburn in the morning when we had to leave each other at the end of a visit. *Literal heart pains* would awaken me from the deep of sleep as I lay next to you, holding your body, your back turned away from me. Waves of tearing, invisible lines inflaming within the wall of my chest released deep throbbing, echoing, and aching.

I thought of my body's responses to unconscious certainties—and heard the words *"gripping fear."* With my eyes open in the dark, luminous dawn, I contemplated if this was just *my difficulty with trusting* as I grew closer to someone.

I knew, also, the pain could be an innate understanding—that this new territory, of supposed middle ground, could somehow break and tear.

That it may be short-lived.

Lovers reenact what's been unresolved in their lives from before. We only discover by moving *in and through* the terrains of vulnerable intimacies whether pursuit of the other will lead to transformation—or to a drowning in the deepened parts of ourselves, only brought to the surface in the presence of each other.

Perhaps it is both.

Having felt the familiar pulling tides of those who eventually recede too far out to reach, I now wonder if our coming together is worth the humility and effort—

> because, though we can heal, as we try to rework these
> patches of discord together in the hope of redemption—
> we can also simply arrive at the same story,
> told over again,
> through the lens of a different unfolding narrative.

⟡

The light we had for a time stood within, like the warmed sun clearing beneath the canopy of the leaves of trees, became cooler.

Through time, the events strung together and formed a more coherent and enduring picture.

I sobbed into the floor, *deep*, bellowing pain, as I further acknowledged what was emerging. Through my protesting tears and pleading, I cried—knowing *there was love here.*

My memories began to flash through images from my past I had hoped to have healed—but which I was uncovering—*perhaps we never fully do.* My relationship with the painter, my family—the drinking, fighting, and fragility. Harsh, egoic defenses from others. Sabotage. Neglect, cruelty, and abandonment.

I screamed tears that howled into the carpet as I despaired the many years I'd spent *trying to work it through, trying to be better, trying, trying, trying to heal . . .*

And here I was, all the same.

We don't always get the yields of love we believe are possible through years of hard wrestling and labor.

Outgrowing our wounding is slow, slow work.

I sat for a long time that afternoon, staring, snot-faced and tear-gazed at the fading light streaming through my kitchen's back window.

I faced, in that moment, the mirror of what I knew was only an extension of my own unresolve: a continuation come to clarify its presence within me through my love with you.

I had reached for this.

And there was still more unattended wounding in me I had not outgrown.

I hung my head in unutterable humility and grief.

You'd given me the insights, like startling pieces of breadcrumbs, appearing as dappled clues on the floor. When the crumbs had become a solid loaf that I tripped over, suddenly, face-planting straight onto the ground, slamming me down, I stayed: face to the floor. And already down, I simply let myself fall into what was real.

I'd just moved into a new apartment that you had helped me look for as part of our future hope to live together sometime in the year to come. You came to visit me that first weekend after moving in. It was then I felt more clearly the shifting within you, more than the trickling I had begun to know and question in the months before.

In you was some sort of whispering withdrawal—a subsiding that I could not quite contact or name, even in the sensing—as you stood before me in the same room.

I sat alone in the bath that weekend.

And knew that truth tends to rise as two people move closer together.

What had been formed between us began breaking and spiraling down, abruptly, only two days after you left.

Considering the story as a whole, maybe it wasn't so sudden.

I listened in a removed sort of posture as your escalating fury reverberated over the phone into a height and perversion I had not yet known, erupting into a defensiveness interlaced with rage and harsh inversion of what I'd just been saying—when I tried telling you something hadn't felt right the weekend before, and asked if we could talk about it, in a soft and even voice.

"You know what," you replied, "don't bring your problems *about me, to me* anymore. I don't want to hear about them."

I sat with the quiet stillness of observation that comes as the preemptive pause that is mobilized to find a moment of reprieve, and used to head off the inescapable grief that will soon succumb to hard reality. I felt myself wonder, naively for a moment, if I could undo the steps—and anxiously take us back to the moments before, when we had still felt close.

Somewhere between the subtle shock of what was happening and the forceful loyalty I held inside my gut to *see this for what it was*, I was left only with the unutterable devastation of knowing I was no longer going to be able to get to you in a way that felt safe.

There was no going back to where we were before.

Perhaps the truth was there was nothing *from before* to get back to—but that this was the picture that really was, all along.

I cried on the other end of the line, knowing what I loved in you was no longer something I could hold onto, along the cliffs of what was falling down, the ground between us that was gone.

I hung up the phone, knowing I was walking away, and moved very slowly the rest of the afternoon.

On my couch in the shadows of leaves outside my window, in a snail-like pace, I sat in heaviness and grief.

By evening, I stood—and walked quietly down my neighborhood street, and made tea in the silence between empty apartment walls.

It was all I could do—to move simply and slowly, with my own sludging, deliberate intention to feel and acknowledge what was real.

I waited for you to reach for resolution, to call back and say *it had been a mistake.*

But the phone never rang.

By night, I sat densely in the chair at my desk. Breath heavy, and slow. Looking at the dropping gold evening light falling farther down peach-colored concrete buildings and reflecting window-sills across the street.

In the heavy, descending, quiet, and clear—

was the intuition.

The knowing.

That same clarity of God.

Today, I stood in the bookstore where we first met. Midmorning sun was pouring brightly through the opened windows above the tall and open, book-filled space, as the smell of an aged building perfumed itself—beautiful cherrywood, shining bright.

Everywhere around me, readers came and went in their busyness.

Timelessness took on its meaning, as the feelings of once awaiting and then meeting you swept up from beneath me. I stood for a while, hovered near the section on *Essays and Criticism*, and stared up the stairway where you'd climbed to meet me that cold day in April.

Turned out they didn't have the book I was looking for the day we met.

They didn't have Joseph Campbell's *An Open Life*.

Time passed, and after a while, my friend caught my eye from the corner behind me, and asked if we needed to leave.

Tears flowed down my face on the sidewalk among the Sunday morning bustle of busy brunch-goers, and I wept for the simple but free feeling of missing you. Crying openly, I felt a feeling of faithfulness toward the tears on my face—

letting them run, I would not wipe them away.

I am not ashamed of my love for you.

And I will not hide what you meant to me.

When she tried to talk to me on the drive home, my head lay back peering out the window, and I did not want to move from the ache in my heart to the thoughts of my head. No renditions of *It could be better.* or *What is it exactly that brought this on?* could save me from what I so longed to feel near me again—

the memory of you and I, emerging from distance to closeness to meet that early spring morning, and the continuing of a journey together that we would, for a time, have in the comfort of what was ours.

I don't find that it is complicated, as we drive along the shore of this crisp beachfront near my home. The air and the sun, and your absence, are real.

I feel gratitude that I can feel what I do, that I can feel the realness—anything at all, in the ache you left which echoes what has been mine all along.

I know what it conveys.

Mark Knopfler sings a song with *Dire Straits* on the radio. And I think of our song together, not yet fully sung.

How far do you think we've come, since our knowing, loving, and parting? Do you believe, as I do, that the teachings are still emerging and subsiding, as we forever unfold into what we are to become?

The small gut of my soul still aches for you in the morning, in those first few moments, when the peace of sleep, like the light sheet upon my body, slides away from me—and reality, in its heaviness and air, settles down upon my skin. Attachments are not so easily defined or undone, despite whatever naming we can conjure to help us understand their meaning. Our souls overlapped and then tore in the leaving, and I now face the reality—

as each day passes,

and you are in fact no longer by my side.

Like I said, it's not complicated.

I loved you.

And I'm sad that you're gone.

Love is not only about the wounds.

But we cannot run from ourselves, you and I.

"I want the deeper healing to occur."

You said this to me once. We were standing beneath tall trees, and the loud, echoed roaring of a river cried from beneath us.

I felt resonance with you in that moment, of the many we shared, and I felt beside you.

But more than that—I felt with clarity, the quiet subtlety, and heaviness, of respect.

Perhaps you believed that the way things were could be sustained without the emerging of what lay beneath. Perhaps it was me who did. I love that good in us—the way we long to reach toward each other, believing we can emerge victorious, and create something that exists beyond the pattern of who we once were and now long to become.

I still believe this is where healing can further itself—

on the gentle waters where we experience the fullness of ourselves—

in moments of clarity, unharmed by the inheritances of our past.

When we are in patient relationship with each other.

In these small openings where we wade delicately upon the water, trying something new and seeing if we can remain afloat, is where hope resides.

And then we settle into the sand of where we are meant to stand, feet sinking beneath, as we rock gently among the waves—

and in the specks of light shimmering atop the surface of our shadows, we understand the limitations of where we cannot go.

There is steadiness that comes from our soul's simple and clear draw, no matter what it takes us through. When we follow and come to understand what is ours—

and acknowledge, sometimes, in our leaving—

what are no longer our waters.

You caressed your fingers along the sand-like corner of a page, as I ran mine along my own, legs touching, sitting by your side. Synchronous movement between us. We turned the pages of different books, reading divergently—

together, side by side.

And then, a memory, so holding in its embrace, that transcends from across the distance of what's been left behind—

I love you.

And I You.

Goodnight . . .

With you.

Eternal place . . .

20 Years

— Dad —

After he died, when his heart beat its last beat, and his last breath was released, his wife left the room and a woman asked him, "Are you sailing on your boat, John?"

And although she believed in no god, no higher power or spirit passing from life, through the end, to what is to be—she waited, and in that final moment, saw a smile settle onto his dying face.

Very few times in the years following, I saw that boat, sailing off in the distance, and for no other reason than in wondering thought, I watched it sail away, knowing it was you.

Off in a place that surpasses all time and space.

And as the annual November setting sun sunk deep gray into the clouds, and a seagull blew far away in a chilling autumn wind,

I sat tonight as that boat passed me by in the distance, as if to say "Hello" and "I'm still here."

ᑲᔆ

I hold the memory of you somewhere within the cells of my body.

I've heard this is where we hold the deeper losses that can't be reached. Where our scars echo in silent harbors, as the hurt waits within corners deep inside.

Many of my attempts to get to what happened to me when you left—

no. Died—

have proved mostly resistant.

It's an unusual sensation for me. As someone who lives so much from a place of feeling.

I know the difference within me: between what has been known and therefore can be remembered, and what remains un-accessed and dormant with regard to you. The discrepancy has frustrated and plagued me for years. All the times I have tried to *lean*, to *press against* what is blocked, and barricaded within me . . .

Efforts haven't often yielded much release, or succumbed to very much.

I knew a woman who said, "We need to respect people's de-fenses."

Leaving what feels unfinished alone, as it lays unsettled in qui-escence, can be harder than it might seem.

I almost drowned when I was a little girl.

Walking airily near the ocean, three years old, along the beach near the edge of the waves. Encapsulated within my own spacey thoughts, singing and humming beneath the water-crashing sounds in the air. Bare toes sifting through the small sand, sunlight warming my skin in a salt air breeze.

Beyond the shore, beneath the waves, are unseen worlds—hidden to the naked eye. Beachlines that suddenly sever from the mainland, immediately, and without warning. Dropping quickly over, falling down to the depths of a bottomless ocean floor.

It's the ruminant rhythm of the crashing waves along the shore that relaxes the spirit and distracts the mind from further knowledge of the undertows—lying beneath the surface world. We gaze over the top of the water toward the horizon, assuming in the glistening beauty that everything is alright.

We are safe.

That day, the waves wakened higher, quickening their rolling arch, gaining great strength, and climbing into a rogue.

I couldn't hear you screaming my name from a distance, before I went under—

swept away toward the underwater cliffs—

tossed within the undertow . . .

You came, and pulled me up for air.

When I was seven, I lost my way through a labyrinth of halls in an inn where we were staying in the mountains. You were outside in the jacuzzi with my little brother, Toey, where snow surrounded everything in white. I wanted to go back inside to where Mom lay sick with flu in the floors above, and attempted with an independent, childhood stride, to follow your verbal compass back to the room.

I opened the wrong door and found myself inside a cold and empty room with concrete walls beneath a staircase. The door slammed behind me. I heard it echo through hollow space, and turned, frightened—to see there was no handle in order to get out. I flattened my small hand on the door, then pounded, standing, dripping wet in my swimsuit, screaming, wailing for someone to let me out.

The room reverberated with my screams; no one could hear.

Panic almost became me, and my eyes widened and darted from side to side, as I realized: *I could forever be stuck inside this room.*

Freezing and shaking.

Nothing but a pool of water dripping from my swimsuit into a puddle of wet on the floor beneath my feet.

I was brought close to the same edge as those ocean shores that almost dragged me toward a droppage into something unknowable, too big to be ignored, despite my resistance to confronting its enormity and presence—

when the door flung open, and you ran in to get me.

Perceptions of failure unfold on multiple levels, dropping us layer by layer to the floor like the wilting petals of a dying flower.

I entered the room of your coming death with an awkward movement, stiff, and quiet, in a stifled hospice, where the midafternoon light of fall settled gray between dim layers of a window, which blurred my eyes. The sight was both dull and blinding. Beneath the window of sickened light, an unraveling woman sat facing the bed, with the hunched-over figure of a desperate and tearful boy leaning heavily into her side.

I tried to adjust my eyes from disillusionment to reality, never fully making the destination. I looked at the bed and felt the person beneath its sheets could have been anyone but a person I knew. Guarding, disconnecting sick atrophies of emotion became me as I looked upon the skin—stretched, oily, like a mustard-colored tourniquet pulled tightly across the faucets of a face, and a jaw that hung open with rasping, fluid-drowning breaths. The face, once familiar, was now distorted with an unfamiliar, yellow, shining glow of death.

Beneath the descending body, I saw the semblance of you, who you once were. And I knew that it was you—and that the woman crying in quiet hysterics was my mother, and that the child beside her was my brother. And that it was all real, and it was happening. That in this quiet and anesthetized moment, morphine dripping wet into the collapsed vein of your arm, this unfamiliar place of inauthentic expression and suffocation was to be our last.

Capacity for genuine feeling exited my delicate thirteen-year-old body as quickly as I had entered the room and was replaced instead by an automated, robot-like response:

Sit down.

Take dad's hand—

uncomfortable.

Glance at mother and brother—

crying.

Look to Dad—

can't speak.

Look at own hand—

uncomfortable.

Gently move thumb, attempt genuine gesture . . .

Blink. Tears. Blink.

Can't speak. No words. Can't breathe. Something in my throat . . .

"I love you."

A voice inside that whispers: "Not enough."

Want to say more. Want to say more. Say more, say more, say more . . .

Can't.

I think at one point I imagined my last words to you would be something remarkable, meaningful.

I'm sorry they weren't.

How do you introduce the story of a dead father in his daughter's life?

How do you truly own it when it's yours?

Holding the grief of others is often easier than acknowledging our own.

Life opens short moments to release the flood—I remember how I screamed, broke the glass of that picture I framed of you and Toey and I, and told you: *I hated you.*

Told you it was *all your fault*—that life had ended up as it had.

I screamed out loud, ripe, bellowing rage. And cried gut-clenching tears that late afternoon on my knees.

When you were alive was the short time in life when I didn't have to ask for what I needed.

The way you made me breakfast, before driving to work at the hospital in the cold, black morning by yourself. My eyes blinked open, and I jumped from my bed, hoping to catch you before you left. Running to my window, I saw the tailpipe of your red Saab blow white, puffing clouds into the air as the gears shifted, and you drove away.

I felt the dip of disappointment, even then. Knowing I had missed something—some moment, that was never to return.

But then I went downstairs, and found you had left the kitchen lights dimmed down low, and the oven was warm and cracked open, slightly ajar. Barefoot in a nightgown, cool floor beneath my feet, the kitchen quiet, I peered into what I knew was inside— *"Bun-on-the-Run"*—bacon, egg, cheese on an English muffin, wrapped in tinfoil.

Breakfast, just for me.

⌃

Bringing a neck brace for someone in an accident who held no insurance. Giving work to a struggling teen. Overpaying babysitters.

Beneath your giving sat an awkward loneliness at times, and there were moments I sensed you were embarrassed, and didn't know how to *be.*

Something rippled, and I felt shame that *broke my heart.*

The way *you gave*; wanting me to dance or ride. You encouraged me to *go* and *live.*

But I didn't want to leave you alone in your sadness.

So many powers at play.

I sat beside you in the car at nine years old, jerking from the thrust of a rear-ended bump at a neighborhood stoplight—when you glanced in the mirror, yelled in a whisper, "Fucking bitch!" toward the rumpled driver behind, who was just sixteen.

I watched you and Mom interlace your relationship with something unkind, where accruals of biting sarcasm had nowhere else to go than from tendrils of subtle remarks to escalations of fury.

Never will I forget the day she ran naked around the house while you chased her, and then spat in her face.

I trembled, held Toey, called the police—

then was yelled at by Mom, for exposing

what was already there.

You apologized a day later, after the frenzy had found its way back to homeostatic norm—

but I wouldn't look at you, for the anger and sadness at

what you had betrayed.

⌒⍥

You died.

For months after, your office stayed the same.

I remember how I watched the stillness of the room, listened to the faintly *swishing* grandfather clock in the kitchen. "Virgil," Mom called it. She was always naming things.

Stacks of papers and bills scattered over your oversized mahogany desk. Your chair, empty, in front of it. I heard it squeak, in the memory of you shifting, alone at your desk, late at night. Working.

Old dirty pennies and a couple of nickels sat clumped together on the wood panel, once a window frame, that separated your office from the living room. Next to them, a thin, black pen, still capped, and your black, waxy-smelling Chapstick. Remnant items of your daily life that once filled your pockets.

Now they were only scatterings that signified your presence had once been something real.

It was funny—the small, simple things that were missed.

I missed the sound of you removing all the remnants of your daily living, and the way it told me you were home.

Pen sliding from your jeans, change dropping on the desktop.

I stared—trying to gather some life from their now empty, meaningful existence.

They sat blankly, did little to amend what I was reaching for.

That afternoon, the phone rang in the kitchen. One single ring sounding through the still of the house. I crossed my arms, hugged myself in your study, let it ring. The sun felt warm through the windows, and the stillness calmed and dropped me beneath the thoughts of my mind.

"You've reached four-two-five, eight-eight-five, one-one-two-nine. We're not here to take your call, please leave a message."

It was your voice. One room away.

Beep.

"Hello, this message is for John Kemp. My name is Amy, and I'm calling from The Seattle Times . . ."

I shot across the room as if I had floated from one place to the next. My hand gripped the phone, trembling in anger, or excitement—of what? I didn't know.

"This is Christina Kemp."

The tone in my voice was much older than the years in my bones.

"Oh, hello Ms. Kemp, my name is Amy, and I'm calling about John Kemp's newspaper subscription to The Seattle Times."

My heart raced; an anger elevated within my chest.

"The person you're looking for is dead. He died last week." I cut her off, bluntly.

Honestly . . .

It was true?

I wanted to see what she would do. I allowed the statement to hang in the air. I had been curious those days, as I waited to see how people would or wouldn't respond after hearing of your dying, as they clumsily or gracefully attempted to thread the patch of death that couldn't be mended. Most of the responses were awkward attempts to scurry around the pain. Ineffectual. Uncomfortable. Inauthentic.

I was always disappointed.

I waited, longing to hear resonant words of comfort. But instead, found only the overwhelming incompetence of adults around me.

Why are you the one who's uncomfortable? I always wondered.

The telemarketer began her response, "Oh, my gosh, I . . . I apologize Ms. Kemp. We were not made aware . . ."

I felt my shoulders soften, as I sensed her sorriness and compassion, not meaning to cause harm or disruption, and I released my grip on the phone—sorry, and tired.

I rubbed my eyes.

"It's fine. Can you please remove him from your list? Thank you for calling . . ."

I clicked off the phone and set your absence down on the counter.

On that counter were incongruous items and papers—grocery lists on the backs of envelopes, old credit card bills, unopened mail with coffee stains, utilities unpaid, notes and scribbles from months passed. A tiny Dosinia shell sat beside a chewed, blue pen cap. The pen was nowhere in sight.

I slid my fingers over everything as if to sway and swirl them together, trying to see what I could feel. For a moment, I remembered my hand hovering above the cold water of the San Juans as I leaned over the side of our dinghy to feel the air above the water. We'd gone out at dusk as a family, only a few years prior, before your cancerous dying had encroached us all. The cold massiveness of the overwhelming oceanic body of water was just beneath my hand, creaking and moving the floor of the dinghy with the waves beneath it . . .

The enormity of that water frightened me sometimes.

I realized I had stopped breathing—and looked back upon the layers of mail. Underneath a few bills, I saw your handwriting, a note you'd left for Mom some morning before going to work at the hospital.

"Have a good day, be home tonight—I'll call you on my way. Love, JK."

Your notes were always scattered over some counter all over the house. You left one for Mom every day.

There would be no more notes, now.

My middle finger hovered over the words, but I would not touch the paper.

I stood for a moment, in the house where no one was around, presence amid an emptiness, and my hand lifted to softly touch the side of my face. I wrapped my hand behind the back of my neck, and felt the pressure of touch offer something like release.

I moved and walked through the dusty hallway, where dog hair sat clumped together in a thin line along the floorboard moldings and beneath the pantry closet. The light of the laundry room window flooded through and heated the small space of the end of the hall as I reached for the rusted doorknob of the back door, turned and heard *that familiar, rusted, squeaky sound,* and stepped onto the cool floor of the garage where the large door was lifted open, showing life outside. The warmth of the midafternoon sun shone over the driveway and the trees, and atop your dust-covered Saab. I walked over the cold, smooth, garage floor, and onto the driveway, where the tiny pebbles gently grated the pads of my bare feet, where each step was a solid force of focus and a floating movement all at once.

In the heavy place of distillment, where the undercurrent is what leads, I looked over the driveway, neighbor's yard, and then our own sloping green.

A few birds were singing somewhere in the near distance.

The quiet from inside the house followed me—as I walked toward your car, placed my hand on the black handle of the passenger seat, pressed my thumb into the knob, and gently opened the door.

I climbed inside the warm, sunlit encasement, slid onto the beige leather passenger seat, closed the door, leaned my head into my hand, and exhaled a single long moan of tears.

The first anniversary of your death I tried to "remember you thoughtfully," and grieve.

I was fourteen at the time. The remembrance was a forced sort of self-perpetuated ceremony; I held the wooden, Buddhist beads you wore around your neck sometimes, and the picture of our family in the setting sun of our backyard, taken by the professional photographer friend who borrowed and then stole the Cannon camera you had left to me. The photo was taken just before you became noticeably, cancerously ill, and I guess you and Mom had wanted to preserve some idea of our family.

What was it you wanted us to remember?

I sat trying to pull together some sort of ritual to honor, remember, and mark your passing—whatever it was that people did when someone died and went away.

It felt wrong not to try.

Still, I didn't know what to do.

Sitting alone on the floor in my room, heater blazing over my crossed legs . . . knowing that no one really wanted to remember with me . . . Mom, somewhere out of the house, and Toey, locked away in his room.

I wrote a poem, instead, months later landing inside the thin, small pages of some anthology somewhere on the east coast of the country.

Where has he gone?

You look in the breeze, when the branches sway, and the leaves fall
silently to the ground.
You look in the swiftly moving clouds, as they move calmly across the
brightened blue sky;
but there is no one there to be seen, or heard.
Maybe in the grass, or behind the old oak tree?
But no, just empty, lifeless things;
waiting, watching,
there to pull and grasp you into an illusion that doesn't exist . . .
You believe that when you look in a flaming fire, that you can see him,
or on the water, moving beneath a pale blue moon—
that you can feel him, touching your skin, breathing life into you, urging
you and helping you,
to go on.
But what is this, what we believe we feel, or see, or hear?
Is it just the relentless fear that we are now empty, alone?
Should we believe in the illusions that we see,
should we forever hold him in our hearts,
follow our hearts?
Or should we wait, for the right time, to just let go . . .

Mom said she could "still feel you."

It reminded me of the way I watched people in films be visited
by their parents after they'd died, and the otherworldly narratives
of books I had read.

I waited through the years for you to make yourself known to
me in the same way, figuring your ghostly return would indicate

my value was enough for you to transcend the limits of the ethe-real to be with me, nearby.

One afternoon later that spring, the small TV that sat atop the kitchen counter turned on from across the room where I stood, out of nowhere.

"Dad?"

Nothing.

"Dad."

Nothing.

I collapsed onto my stomach on top of my bed in the afternoon following school that spring.

The tears evidenced some inner faucets opening—but the connection remained obscure, despite the choking, gasping, and cries. Like the feeling of not fully feeling. Like the strange, anes-thetized sensation of topical numbing—of not being able to push through the general surface to the inner land of what's really been torn apart.

In absence of being tangibly informed by an authentic landing, I tried on rambling attempts to understand, hoping my words would glean some truthful insight into how I felt. What left my mouth were utterances of contempt which, said out loud, made me sick to my stomach.

I'm sorry, I'm sorry, I'm sorry. I'm sorry.

I'm sorry.

I'm sorry.

Over-responsibility in the lacking face of containment and no assistance in the making of meaning. The statement felt both real and largely untrue, all in one, same surge. Like a shredded attempt to find fragmented emotional truth and relief.

Pleading.

Just tell me what I did wrong.

Hand pounding the bed.

I just did something wrong!

Desperation.

Just tell me what it is . . .

Misaligned guilt, and refusal to let go—

Just come back, and I'll do better . . .

I bundled myself in the tight enclave of a ball.

Eventually, my two best friends found their way into my room and sat beside me as I lay in my tears.

It never occurred to me at the time—

that it might have been Mom who called them . . .

When I was eighteen, my last year at home, I went looking through your desk in your office for something from you—anything—that would have been left intentionally behind.

I sunk inside when Mom told me that you had written goodbye letters to all of your colleagues at the hospital, but not left a single one for anyone in our family.

"He just couldn't, sweetheart . . ."

I'd scrambled through your oversized desk, envelopes, bills, letters sliding around, drawers open and me lifting and peering and scattering through the useless legibility of your handwriting on white pieces of paper—I did so because I couldn't believe that you would just forget me. That you would just die, and leave nothing behind for me to hold onto.

Something in me had remained faithful to the belief that you would never die without saying goodbye.

I searched, and gave up searching, for words you never took the time to say.

ᏨᏍ

I made my way through the world after I moved out of the house. Studied pre-medical sciences and psychology, worked in a hospital with cancer patients, lived in an apartment in the city . . .

One day at a tea shop in my early twenties, a girl in my periphery, about my age, sat at a wood-checkered table across from her father, and I overheard her discussing her college classes, boyfriend, and summer plans.

The two of them caught my eye from where I sat at my normal table by the window, as the low murmurings of people chatting and sipping their steamed cups echoed throughout the room, and they laughed and held nibbled pastries that left traces of crumbs atop the tables. I was leaning over a stack of papers and a textbook on some prerequisite for graduate studies I wanted to pursue, even though applying was still years away.

When the pull of their presence took me away from my study, I watched them, and was struck by something I couldn't name—

as I observed them sitting closely together, laughing. They were so familiar and engaged. Just a girl engrossed in her own life, staring wide-eyed at her father's opinions, when they were offered, sparingly, in thoughtful response to her seemingly normal life predicaments.

I stared, completely absorbed and in awe, and I became suddenly aware of my inability to link anything in my experience to what I was watching.

A warmth, and normal exchange, between father and daughter that humidified the air.

What a foreign land, I thought to myself, biting the tip of my pen cap.

I gathered my things and left the tea shop that day, ashamed.

I often drove the strand that stretched along the waterfront beyond the city while I was in my twenties. One year in early summer, when I was twenty-five, I glimpsed another of your boats, white-capped and sailing in the distance.

I parked near the tip of the beach beside the lighthouse, where the road curved away from the bustle of the main drag and sat overlooking nothing but islands far in the distance over smooth, rolling waves of blue. I closed the door to the car, walked over to the railing that separated onlookers from the sound, warm in the sun, where salt danced in the mild wind that blew off the water.

I wasn't there for anything in particular—just a moment of reprieve, some reset from the day. I felt lonely relief to be near the water, with its familiar faithfulness that always spanned through the years.

Something steady through my life that I needed had stayed.

I leaned into the steel rail and breathed in the air.

I stood for a while, as couples walked their dogs at the end of the day and a jogger passed me by. Some seagulls floated above and landed, flapping together, on the rocks along the shore.

Something sudden and quiet arose from a place I could not discern, and I sensed an essence around me:

I stood erect, eyebrows furrowed, and pressed my hands into the rail—

and knew in that instant . . . that it was *you.*

An inescapable familiarity overcame me, and I felt you with me, *alive* as you had ever been. I looked around to sense where you might be coming from—

and down in the water, I sensed it was in the *waves.*

I stared, as the small wakes began to splash in an enlivened rhythm, speaking a new sound. And I couldn't help but *laugh* from some unfiltered, childlike place of wonder, as I began to feel the most playful and fullest kind of joy—

with my hands on the rail, I stood fully erect and tall, and held your presence, openly.

The moment would not pass,

as a wave swept away, with its withdrawing, miniscule pause,

then lapped back in again, and I still felt you near.

For an instant, I became afraid—that in the rescinding,

your presence in the water would disappear—

and I held my breath anxiously, wondering if you would return.

With each new lap against the concrete wall, you returned. And I felt you stay with me, there, in that simple, unanticipated moment.

As the waves swept back-and-forth in a resurgence of watery speaking, you kept splashing, and I smiled and laughed as you crashed again up against that manmade wall by the sea—and I knew in a knowingness that exists deep beneath thought: that it was you.

I remained, and released my spirit into a peaceful embrace of unseen holding.

As the waves died down, I felt you linger, and while your presence softened but remained, I looked to my right at the enormity of the sun,

setting before me in the sky.

I felt God, too, in that moment, and what was said rang true and clear:

You are alright. We are right here—and you are alright.

You were still lapping, gently, softly in the sea. Quietly lingering against the walk . . .

The next afternoon, I was diagnosed with stage II malignant melanoma.

Standing in the office where I was a research assistant for a study on chronic pain, I gripped the phone, as I heard the words "it is cancer" from my doctor on the other end of the line.

A tear dripped down my cheek as I stared at the study logo on a magnet: a white sailboat tilting on the water in the wind.

I guess my grief, unmetabolized, found another way to make itself known—in that small, amorphous mole on the space between my shoulders on my back.

Your cancer had been there, too.

You were an anesthesiologist, and I was working in the Department of Anesthesiology.

Now, we had the same cancers, in the same locations—just different years apart.

The only difference between you and I—and I suppose it is marked—is that my cancer was cut out, and today I am fine, barring the six-inch scar I now carry on my back.

But you never made it out of what couldn't be removed, eradicated, or cured, did you Dad?

Like I said, I carry the memory of you in the cells of my body.

But I do appreciate that brief visit from you, all the same.

I wonder about the span of our experiences—from the existential to the ordinary . . .

Through most of my life, I've had to discern where the meaning lies without your help.

I pressed my foot atop the clutch of your car,
    learning to drive when I was sixteen—
      and my attempts to maneuver through seasons
        were a bit clunky for a time.

Living holds some difficult transitions—
    but I've begun to figure out
      how to shift the gears more smoothly.

I still remember the difficulty, though—
    through so many years,
    of finding those rhythms.

I've hated you at times for leaving me with so little to *feel, remember,* and *hold onto.*

Today, I wonder: which of those is really yours for me to blame?

There are words you could have said, that could have remained, even when you went away. People always say we should *know* how much our parents love us . . .

But in the silent pages, so much of what is offered is only another person's attempt to compensate for lost comfort.

I can take responsibility for what is mine to locate and hold onto:
    but I needed to hear from you—
    the way you loved me.

Today, it's been over twenty years since you died.
    Sometimes, I connect to the longings I still have for you—
      that make themselves known from time to time,
      and arise mostly in moments that are simple.

When I remember:

The way you carried me asleep in your arms when I was a little girl.

Or—

    how you offered me your sleeve to wipe my nose on when I cried.

I *knew* you were happy to see me—

    because of the intonation in your voice when you greeted me as I
    came home from school.

I had semblances of knowing once before,

    somewhere in my being:

That you would be there for me if things ever really went wrong.

I sink to deepened waters within myself, sitting on the hard front porch of my house—snot pouring from my nose and wet tears drenching my clenched, closed eyes. And I draw my hands tightly together, and drop my head, and know with rageful mourning:

There are simple things that I still need from you.

To tell me: *I can do this.*

That I am *something good.*

How I will *forever,* in a *boundlessness, be loved.*

And that I *can,* even when it's hard—

    always find my way.

Gazing across the grass, I wipe my nose on my own shirt sleeve, and suppose we never stop needing our parents—

    and we never stop grieving their loss, do we?

I cannot always stay connected to the lines.

    And I am again carried away from the anchoring hold.

    Somewhere in the drift, I'll get to you, I'm sure—

        because we're never so far from what we want to avoid.

No matter our defenses:

We cannot outrun what we are meant to heal.

So many ropes to untangle from the docks—they are the knots
you never taught me to untie.

Life is full of many things: simple, contradictory, dis-eased,
mysterious—

all that is ordinary, wonderful, and obscure.

Being here is a wave to contend with.

I wonder if I'll live true,

to the life inside, my heart fully longs for . . .

Rocking back-and-forth on the boat between the docks.

Turning and swaying beneath the mast.

The Creek

— Margaret —

I'm kicking rocks in the dirt, as our shoes scuff the gravel on the road.

No words are spoken, but what is said is not unheard. In the quiet sensing between friends, we often know what others cannot. At eleven years old, I am contemplating and serious—and then, it comes.

"Nobody knows what they have until it's gone . . ."

I speak this into the afternoon air, then stop on the road—and you follow. Pausing, we turn to look back at my old house, standing with deep green trim, cedar shingles, and sunlit front porch amid surrounding acres of trees. It is the house my dad built and then had to leave behind when we moved next door to you—this year, at the beginning of sixth grade.

Brightened rays from the sun attempt to peek through in small, shallowed openings of light but disappear through the thick evergreen branches. Shadows play where we stand on the small dirt road, beside the clusters of trees whose young trunks stretch thin and tall toward an atmosphere hidden from our sight.

Something about voicing what has been stirring down beneath the surface brings to light what might have otherwise remained untouched, abandoned as pieces of unclaimed life lost to the ethers.

I feel a sad aching and nostalgic remembrance in the one simple acknowledgment.

We continue walking a little further, when beside me you say, "I think you should write about it."

"About what?" My eyebrows are furrowed; I am still condensed in my thoughts of feelings.

"What you just said—
the way nobody knows what they have 'til it's gone."

A grass hill slopes through the backyard of a yellow-painted country home, turning golden in the late September setting sun. At the bottom stands a maple tree in the lower corner of the yard. The sound of a rope swing stretching and drifting through its leaves mimics the laughter of two girls swinging and playing in the early evening sunlight. One is seated on an old wooden-planked seat of the swing, while the other runs by her side, shoving off the ground to cast them into motion, jumping onto the other's lap midair.

The rope's sound changes, as it is pulled with new weight. My stomach lifts, and my arms are filled with the tingling, excited rush of flight.

We glide to new heights.

A familiar voice echoes from your house next door. "Dinner!"

Seconds later, from my own back porch, my mother calls me by nickname, "Anna, come and wash your hands for supper!"

Off we run, shouting that we'll see each other tomorrow morning at the bus for school.

And we're gone.

In the fall, one year later, thrown over my shoulder is an old woven Mexican backpack filled with a bag of chocolate chips and two cans of Coke that tap together between the beat of my footsteps that crunch atop the thick gravel road beneath my feet.

Treading with joyful purpose down toward the creek, I turn as you shout, "I'm coming!" and catch up behind me.

In the late afternoon hours after school, we tread down the trail a few more yards, arriving at our destination.

Walking in small, slippery steps down the embankment to the creek's edge, the damp earth rises fragrantly around us, and our sandals sink slightly into the wet mud as we near the water, where small lapping sounds beside the cool, streaming current.

Stepping carefully into the gently motioning water, we wade momentarily.

"It's cold," I say.

From behind me the small overpass of a damp bridge shades the air and creek. I look at you for reassurance, measuring your reaction to the temperature.

"Yeah."

You look down creek in the opposite direction, scoping the path ahead.

We wade for a moment, allowing our feet and legs to adjust to the briskness, and begin making our way. Downstream in the rushing current, we quiet our voices as we pass the backyard of the old man who once yelled at our presence in the water. "You'll kill the salmon spawning! Get out of there!" We'd giggled, and rushed to get away . . .

Each step is a careful pilgrimage along the smooth and round, slime-encased rocks. You take the lead, stretching out a hand to steady me, as I wobbily attempt to keep from falling from the pressure of the quickly streaming water surrounding my stick-thin legs. We laugh, talk about people from school, and gossip about the latest afternoon rumors before falling into momentary pockets of silence.

The air is filled with the trickling sound of streaming water, and the birds singing a softly fading evening song. The sight of the old wooden bench appears, secretly discovered during our previous trip down creek, sitting peacefully and damply beneath the overgrown brush.

We've arrived.

I slap my backpack down on the bench, and remove our snack as we sit for a while, tossing handfuls of chocolate chips into our mouths and replacing one sugary treat for another with the slurp and swallow of a lukewarm can of Coke. Our legs glide and splash through the clear, green-blue stream. You let out a sigh as a mosquito lands for a meal on your arm, and a slap of skin smacks into the air. I look up into the world of surrounding trees, beginning to darken in the shade, as the sun dips lower and lower in the sky.

When I look down into the water once more, now darkened, almost black, I remain with the stillness. In the ease of waters flowing beneath the glassy surface, I am dipped into the quiet corners of being. Moments go by, and with each passing, I am longing to stay where we are without the movement of time.

My subtle disappointment exists in the anticipation of knowing— *This too will soon pass.*

Brief moments of comfort, so many of them, and feelings and sensations so transient, had led me to this understanding, innate in my youthfulness, so long ago.

Closing my eyes, I release a slow, deep breath. I want to stay the way we are, though I can feel, even before it arrives, what is coming. A subtle angst hovers within my stomach.

"We'd better get going. I need to get home for dinner."

A weight dips into my heart and stomach, and I sigh, a slight wincing in my heart, wishing we could stay longer.

Just stay.

I allow my eyes to focus from the water to my feet once more. Goosebumps are beginning to rise on the top of my legs, and when my own stomach grumbles at the mention of real food, I want to push my hunger aside, in loyalty to deeper longings.

We collect our things, and slowly wading, I lag a little further behind as we make our way back upstream. Thick cold and tingling prickle through my frozen calves and numbing toes as I lift my legs heavily out of the water, one last time.

Mud slurps with the releasing pressure of our feet on the damp earth by the creek. Tired and achy, I press up the small, inclining slope, igniting myself on the brief-but-steep terrain back toward the trail leading away from the creek.

Back on the trail, walking up the dirt and gravel behind our houses, we collect dust onto bare legs and pebbles into wet shoes as we go. They dig into my bare feet, and I miss the soothing cool of the creek as I shake my foot every few steps, trying to free the pinching pressure of a rock from my skin.

The air is settling with an early chill of evening, which smells clean and crisp as I hear the echo of my two dogs from the backyard. We pass their wagging tails and distracting barks and hop over a ditch onto your grass lawn. With your house next door to mine, I veer left and motion through the hemlocks for my driveway.

"Bye Poopy."

"Bye Chrissy Poo!"

When people ask me how we met, I always tell them we were on separate paths, until one day while we were walking, we were funneled together, side by side.

Two sixth graders, brought together by passing classmates and forces unseen, walking together as if they had been meant to find each other all along—

living in houses planted right next door,

as if it were always meant to be.

"Hey, I just moved next to you!" I said.

It was like the universe gently swept us together before the knowledge of our need for each other could take hold.

Some, I believe, would call it Providence . . .

You have straight, brown hair, mine is wavy blonde, and both of us have blue eyes. Back when we were kids, your feet were a size ten next to my thin and narrow five, and your height stood three inches taller than my short and smaller frame.

After we became friends, we were an instantaneous part of each other's lives—always crossing in and out of our neighboring homes.

I was afraid of being outdoors in the blackness at night, with no lights to look for and to find comfort from on our dark, country roads. When I would walk back from your house after playing, I was always anxious and alert. Under the single light of your front porch, I asked you to stay standing at the door until I made it home, shouting, "Are you still there?" every time I made it halfway toward my house, by the ditch at the top of the driveway.

"Yeah. Still here," you always responded back.

Sloughing and scuffing in your oversized sneakers that I'd borrowed having run over in my bare feet, I'd shuffle down the pavement, frightened by what could be lurking in the unseen.

When I made it to the front door, I opened the screeching screen and yelled tepidly that I'd made it, afraid to wake whatever resided in the dark. And then, I waited . . .

"K. Night."

You were always still there.

We walked to our elementary school together through the woods one early winter morning the first year we became friends. It was an adventure to do something different, not to catch the bus up the hill to school, and we woke at the peak of dawn just before morning light to begin our expedition. In freedom and childhood independence, we set out with our plans to navigate through the backstreets and woods, and arrive within the walls of our elementary school at seven-fifty, on time.

My dad made us breakfast and left it in the oven, while I brought Carnation hot chocolate I'd left in thermal cups on the counter the night before, and you took care of the route through the woods.

Cold and crisp in the winter morning, our fingers were numb within oversized gloves and our backpacks clunked, full of books and thick ringed binders, hanging low and heavy as they pounded against our backs with each step over the small twigs and dried, snapped branches on the bed of the forest.

Halfway through our journey, my initial enthusiasm waned as the novelty dispersed with the lifting morning mist, and the light of sun continued raising.

"This is a long walk," I said.

"Yeah," you said back.

"When do you think we'll be there?" I tried to sound in wonder, trying not to whine.

"I don't know. Probably less than twenty minutes," you said—even though you didn't know.

When we arrived in those overheated walls of our sixth grade classroom, our legs were heavy, our clothes were damp from the inside out, and our eyes hung tired, from beneath the early morning hour.

We were just in time for the bell.

I always came into your house through the side door of the garage—and made sure to remove my shoes, because your carpet was clean and vacuumed every day.

Being able to come inside without having to knock made me feel as if I had a special privilege in your house, a home that seemed more formal than mine.

Back then, I came to you first—was always the one to reach and make contact. To ask: "Hey, do you wanna play?"

Your life always had more structure than mine. You had your chores and homework to do, and then had to be back in time for dinner. No one really checked my schoolwork, and whatever chores there were to do were done sporadically and with little follow-through.

I think the truth was that I was afraid in those days—

that if I didn't reach for the connection between us,

what was there might not exist anymore.

That the friendship might fray, and dwindle, and somehow disappear . . .

I'm not sure I trusted that things might survive if I didn't do something to keep them alive.

Also—I was impatient, and didn't want to wait to see if you could play, preferring to just get on with the plans for the day.

But, I think it is also true—
that I was always more open with my needs
than you were.

My leg dangled outside of an open window as I sat on the wooden windowsill in my bedroom, leaning against the frame. Looking over the grass of my front yard with a tin can held to my ear, I listened as your voice muffled something from behind the trees and I strained to understand what I couldn't fully hear.

We ditched our tin-can telephones that fall at the beginning of seventh grade, and bought walkie-talkies instead, so that we could talk to each other from our bedrooms in the hours around school.

Free to communicate *on our own terms*, we no longer needed to pass the telephone through the mediating lines of siblings or parents.

"Are you there? Over . . ."

"I don't get my chemistry homework. Over."

"Roger. I'll be there in five."

We clicked the walkie talkies off, marching across lawns toward each other in patterns that carved a path in the ground of our lives for years . . .

My house was farm-like with loud voices, open windows without screens, flies on the living room walls, and overly vibrant yellow paint with slightly incompatible forest green frames. Next to yours—crisp white, black-trimmed, and colonial, with a kind of silence at times burdened with its own demand—my house seemed even louder.

We rolled through the ditches outside after school, and ran over our grass backyards to hide behind maple trees and rows of small hemlocks when we played with our two younger brothers, who were also best friends. "Bang, Bang!" we shot sounds across the air, and dropped to the ground.

Like the ties formed between people in actual war, what we eventually endured in the hardships of our youths together—
screaming voices from my house
beside dismissive tones from yours—
forged its own kind of bond through the years.

Dying of cancer can take time, and be like a game of stop-and-go.

In the year-and-a-half of uncertainty since his diagnosis, we began to mark when my dad would be in the "really dying" phase by his transition into hospice.

I waited those early fall weeks at the beginning of eighth grade as Dad grew sicker, turning anxiously every time a student helper came into a classroom with a message from the office. When finally, that early November day, the note was for me.

"Christina, your dad is being moved to hospice. Please come to the office. A friend of the family is here to take you home from school."

I had prepared for the moment in my mind over and over in the year before. Despite my premeditative efforts to meet the doom with grace and collected feelings, my body didn't respond as evenly as I had imagined.

The thin layer of stretching polyester fabric from my skirt made me cold, and I found myself regretting not having worn my usual attire of baggy jeans and a sweatshirt, as I went looking for you frantically through the freezing outdoor hallways of the junior high. Opening doors to classrooms, mazing through one after the other; I knew your schedule by heart, but still couldn't find you that morning—and thought—

Why had I decided to dress up?

Three tries, three different classes—

Why wasn't I getting it correct?

When I finally opened the right door, your teacher and I locked eyes, before I saw you seated in the middle back row between a sea of students, and asked if I could please see you outside—

and I remember how *everybody stared.*

The look on my face said that something was up—so when I said it out loud, "the moment" had come—it probably came as no surprise. I left to go to the counseling office, where my dad's doctor friend who we'd spent holidays with was there to take me home.

Later, I heard about the students who flocked to you when the class bell let out and bombarded you with questions and intrigue about whether or not everything was okay.

You managed their intercepting questions, some with genuine concern and others with mutable, short-spanning interest.

It was only later that I imaged the aftermath of what you sorted through.

The way you organized chaos so well.

The identities we unknowingly take up as children can ripple through our lives for years that long outlast our childhoods, until we are ready to redefine them.

Until then, each person is assigned a part to play, and we take on the roles without ever realizing the limitations they impart. Someone is—

The smart one.

The pretty one.

The collected one.
The sensitive one.
The strong one.
The comedic relief.

We learn to steer away from what we might otherwise explore in an expansion of ourselves, for fear we may be treading on the other's terrain.

Our susceptibility to this sensitivity was unavoidable, when both of our homes wouldn't hold us for all that we were. Where we came from related more to scarcity than plenty—making the parts of ourselves that longed to be seen yearn to be reflected back to us in the eyes of others in a way that is so natural and necessary.

We learned to rescind exploring parts of ourselves. And so: *I won't try out for drama, because that's her thing—*

Or: *She needs the recognition this time, so I'll hold back—*

And: *You do "this" and I'll do "that"*

became the thoughts that guided our course,
as we each tried to support the other while we looked
for places to land
that were also ours alone.

But shaping aspects of our identities alongside each other, we also came to rely on each other's natural gifts, which were so often lacking in our own circumstances.

You were a stabilizing presence in my family's ongoing instability. You dampened heightened emotions with objective thought. Remained calm while I was in distress. Challenged the falsity of harmful undertones trying to weigh me down from the voices of the people around me that made their way inside my own mind.

I came to you in order to hear you voice the truths I knew deep inside—but could not find reflected back to me in my own home.

I came to you to sort through answers to the questions I needed to figure out—

help with homework, to vent my frustrations about boys, and for the simple relief our friendship provided from my family's binds.

I came to you to be validated.

"My mom said I have ugly legs."

"It's not true."

"Do you think I'm too much?"

"No."

Or, when my high school boyfriend moved away for college, and I cried, still not having resolved the death of my dad, and said, "Everybody leaves me."

You replied, "I'm still here, so that can't be true. Also, he didn't leave—he moved for school. It's not the same thing."

Your rational mind stood beside the overwhelm of my feelings in need of emotional sorting.

We borrow functions from each other, until we are able to grow our own.

ᔕ

After Dad died, when my mom fell further apart, the pantries were often bare, with the refrigerator left full of useless condiments.

There were rarely any snacks after school, and most nights the newly installed antique stove stood cold.

Those years were a time of unacknowledged paradox: between the money my family had inherited from Dad's passing wake, and our newly remodeled kitchen with no consistent food in the house.

People are easily fooled by appearances—and these were the realities left unseen:

I'd go to your house, and grab a glass from the kitchen cabinet, filling it with chipping ice cubes, I then drank gulping glasses of orange juice straight to the bottom of the glass.

Your kitchen smelled like cooked meat and spices, and I knew that at 5:30 p.m., dinner was always on time.

I grew anxious as I stood waiting to see if I'd be asked to stay. Thinking *please ask, please ask,* hoping you would sense my inner desperation, as my eyes looked down to the floor.

One of your siblings usually rolled their eyes in annoyance. *Staying again?*

From years spanning part of my adolescence, thirteen to sixteen years old, a feeling grew that I was too much to deal with, as I trembled a little inside, embarrassed and tense, standing awkward, and still.

Feeling hungry, and deeply ashamed.

A hand-drawn calendar pinned to a sand-colored corkboard above the wooden desk in my bedroom noted the driver's license exams on the day I turned sixteen.

By late winter, just shy of my birthday, I had bought a used Chevy Blazer, and I gazed out my bedroom window to where it sat in the drive, aware of the ability I would have to escape my confined circumstances on the day my birthday came in the spring. I was approaching freedom, and with it, I could make my own way in the world, and I chewed over possibilities as I watched the car shining in the driveway.

I often opened the car doors and explored inside, playing with a routine of whether I should keep the keys in the ignition or put them on a hook I had hung by my bedroom door. I took naps in the front seats that held me like a child in the mid-afternoon heat of after school hours. The smell of new faux-leather birthed associations of lonely but calm responsibility, and the greater freedoms I would have to look after myself.

You'd come through the hemlocks next to the driveway, open the passenger door, and hop inside, too.

Our legs hanging out the open doors, our bodies slumped down and leaning back in the seats, we talked about where we would go as soon as I passed the driver's exam.

To and from school, without needing to get a ride—(obviously).

Lunchtime drive-throughs. The lake. And movies in the city on weekends.

I passed that exam on the day of my sixteenth birthday, and when we drove the quiet nighttime streets of our hometown with the sunroof open and a mix I made ringing music through the speakers in the car, our elbows hung out the windows, and our hands opened, breezing the air.

Weekend trips in the city were followed by long, lazy, meandering drives through old backroads, which stretched out the slow-paced afternoons and delayed our arrivals back home.

We listened to Deanna Carter on the stereo, and sang "Strawberry Wine" at six-thirty in the morning on the way to high school, with your sister and our other best friend slumped in the seats next to us.

We were never into anything extraordinary.

Just two teenage girls who somehow felt too old for their time, who wanted to get away, and have their best friend by their side to get away with.

At home, I watched as people in my house took turns taking the blame for anything and nothing that resembled sense-making, as the roles and faces of who bore the "problem" were tossed by my mother and stepfather inconsistently from one week to the next. *Brother, me, mom, brother, me, stepdad, brother, me.* Disruptive bouts of screaming and shouting followed lengthy deadpan silences in-between.

I didn't know if I had ever considered myself *smart* or *not smart* before, but I knew by that point I had begun to think of myself as stupid. As those teenage years reached their peak, never having enough energy to invest in school and grades to the degree of some of my peers, I went through the motions of attending classes and felt certain parts of my confidence continue to crumble, alongside your 4.0 GPA and AP coursework.

I guess adolescents measure themselves against the qualities of others. Whatever was assigned at my home in regard to my character was never very carefully measured against what I have come to believe actually stood true. Turning to friendship, I saw it reflected: that you were *intelligent, athletic, and funny,* while I was *messy and serious,* but could sing and do drama. . .

All the while, I never realized how I might have been holding back from budding into other aspects of myself, believing that to survive, I needed to fit alongside the people around me in order to make the picture work.

It took time to discover that in friendship, love holds space for all of who we are to grow fully outward—and that strength can beget strength; intelligence, intelligence; and beauty, beauty.

ᕳᕋ

In our relationship together, we learned how to fight amid models at home and from the world—

the teachers who showed us what not to do.

Together, our arguments grew in a curve that developed through the years just as we did. Our willingness to fight with and for each other strengthened the resilience of our friendship. We learned from each other, and in doing so, became more capable in ourselves, as we wove greater aptitudes of sensitivity toward feeling and rational thought into our developing frameworks. From bedroom-window exchanges about hurt feelings across the grass to sitting in cars at college, resolving growth tensions became a battle we pushed in and through with enough endurance to continue propelling forward.

But even in our best efforts to hold onto what exists between us, sometimes chasms can still open up.

As much as we remain the same, we also shift, and in the rolling of time, each person expands and contracts differently when they begin collecting debris to sort through from their lives.

We succumb to the residue in a timing all our own, often as the pressures in our present living become more than we want to bear.

And we change.

In our early thirties, a gap developed between us, as the wakes we explored in the solitary pilgrimage of our own lives led us to different shores. I began standing taller in the aftermath of the analysis of my own struggles.

And I grew tired of tossing lines and igniting the conversation, and finally just walked away.

Two people can have such different experiences of the same thing. The way we are shaped both inside and out, and our metabolization of life's contents is an enigma that has rippled since the beginning of time, as the way we age becomes a wandering all its own.

For a time, blowing through that growing distance between us existed for me greater breaths of respite, from what had become outgrown and stale.

But as time passed, between the longing to remain loyal to what still feels true and to surrender what I perhaps no longer need, I discovered a willingness to simply set the old binds down.

Chosen or fated, what was meant to continue between us remained for me as love that never really extinguished, and many months on the other side of our goodbye, emerged a joining trail that, to this day, we continue to tread.

There is reprieve in surrender.

And always, an opportunity for unattended issues to resift, perhaps to be returned to, at another time.

When I consider the ways in which you and I relate to others, I often experience observing opposite sides of a similar coin.

I see that we each share themes of caring for people we love, with qualities of rootedness—

    layers of bark denoting intention,

        thoughtfulness, integrity,

            consideration, loyalty,

                and a certain longstanding.

Sometimes, the way we live that careful persistence in relationship simply looks different for each of us.

In and through time, though we've stepped together and then apart, a path has been there between us that has found its way. Perhaps this is what it means to have lifelong kinship: to somehow find, again and again, a way toward togetherness amid the separateness and not knowing.

Wading amid that cool, cold creek, salmon spawned, and the two of us, young but old, found our footing—different, but the same. Brown hair and blonde, you steadied my hand, as creek currents swept briskly by—

> and we have steadied each other, many times, in the years since.

It is no small feat.

In a world where dissolvement and disconnect have become the neglected norm—giving up on people is all too easy. We both know—all too well—how the ties we hope will bind can unwind.

There is consciousness in the decision not to take presence for granted—amid some mystical unseen. To hold a hand across the span of so many tides, and to try to hear—whatever it is that might be calling from the other, in the quiet places they cannot always speak.

We've learned: that sometimes we are less successful than others. But I believe what we have is enough.

And, that what is meant for us will always come back into stride.

I know things about you that many will never see or understand, and the same is true for you of me.

There are also shades of each other that we may never know at all.

I've discovered this is always true of who we love. No matter our histories together or the bonds we forge within them.

The real question I ask myself through the years, as I attempt to peel away what's already known, and see what stands before me with fresh, new eyes—

is: how is it that I am to love you well?

As time endures, I often wonder whether there is a right way to be a friend . . .

I read some poet speaking of long roads together travelled, and I think that life is more about the vulnerable uncertain than what we might try to secure through the false ideas of our minds. . .

Even so—this I can say to the best of my ability:

That I will never stop trying to see you.

And I will always be here, should you need to grab hold—

in the places that shake us,

and tremble us,

and swirl.

In our wobbly attempts to stand, in these quick-paced, trickling, creek waters of life.

Wide Open Spaces

— Clara —

When I arrived at the arena, I stepped my worn paddock boots onto the footing, and breathing in fully, felt the tingling sensation of something beneath my stomach.

Cool air perfused my senses with the smell of freshly raked dirt, and everything lay untouched. No one had been down to the ring in the early hours of morning, and there were no sounds in the barn aisles. Over the arena walls, I saw mist moving, rising off the dewy strings of grass.

The day was only beginning, and all that would become still remained undiscovered. Fourteen years old, with an immediacy of the present moment, the gift of the day felt fully alive as the sun peeked through, early in her rising, deep gold and glowing, the sleepiness of the night falling off in hues of vibrant orange. Shining through the rafters of the silent arena, dust playing on rays of life, soon the light would widely open into expanding, broad, warm, and yellow strokes. The skies were clear, a blanket of blue covering the acres of grasses outside so vibrant and green.

The awakening silence of morning hovered amid the earthy grounds, and within the brown, dust-covered walls of that arena lay the promise of *something new* and undiscovered. A simplicity so often lost with time, as the sense of openness that broaches a new day is worn away by hazy thoughts and outworn ideas . . .

I turned on my heels from the arena and walked down the barn aisle, moseying through the grooming stalls, all swept and organized from the day before—brushes, riding tack, and equipment put away. Hopping into the center of the second aisle, I stopped, my posture tall, hands on my hips, and smelled the familiar surroundings.

As I walked down the aisle, I saw stalls lining left and right, and there was still no sign of a single person. The usual bustling of riders lay asleep, like the quiet rafters above, and the only sound I did hear, as I breathed in the leather tack and stall shavings— was the occasional shift or small snort of one of the horses.

"Paaa-trickkk . . ." I said with my intonation high, ringing into the still morning air.

A soft stirring.

"Paatyy . . ."

A large nose protruded first, and then continued to make its way out of the stall door—the full view of his face appeared, bay-colored and turning to look at me down the aisle. I walked toward him, and we watched each other; a slow, uninhibited, warm and joyful smile formed on my face. The sound of my boots stepping atop the concrete silenced as I arrived at the door of his stall, and, holding out my hand for the soft of his muzzle, his whiskers gently brushed and then tickled my extended palm. I laughed and kept my palm open and waited in anticipation of what I knew would soon come next.

His large, wet, bright pink tongue began licking my hand. Slobbery and smoothly sand-like, it continued to explore as I laughed and stroked the white blaze of his face with my other hand until, all salt cleansed from my palm, his tongue now sat dangling and lazy-like between large, smoothly-edged white and yellow teeth.

I laughed again, and patted the side of his neck, an unspoken endearment toward a horse whose quirkiness had a way of echoing my own—the playfulness in me that emerged when I was away from the presence of mockery, hardness, or intrusive glancing. Perhaps in an alignment that signified the presence of our interconnection, he had also begun to develop similar ailments to my own, like the pain in his back that emerged not long after I'd bought him months before—a pain I, too, had been experiencing, ever since my dad had died the year before.

I reached up to brush his thick, black forelock to the side of his face, and stroked his long, soft ears, gently massaging my hand beneath his broad cheekbone, down below his chin, and over the white blaze of hair that ran down the front of his face.

"Good morning," I whispered, and leaned my face into his.

He smelled the way only horses smell. Thick hair with remnants of sweat, animal, barnlike, with the sweet woodiness of stall shavings around him.

Animals have a sensitive knowingness about them, and can sense vital aspects of people. Sometimes in a glance or particular movement, we can begin to see things we have not attended to in ourselves begin to come to light.

People are like this, too, and there are some who offer us something essential in a time of need, when we are further formed and shaped by their presence.

It only takes the presence of one more developed and wiser than we are to secure a bolstering to allow us to withstand the breakages our early years can often impart. Within their loving presence, we are given the instruments to help refine and strengthen our muscular spirit. We drop in when we might otherwise be vigilantly looking out, and begin sensing within ourselves how to better maneuver through life, when to make a slight adjustment within the saddle, or how to brace the weathering elements of changing seasons with resilience. And we begin to further develop an innate intuition inside that just might allow us to embrace the sensitive honesty of feeling that is needed to navigate us authentically through the rest of our lives.

Today, as I write this, I can hear a neighbor's horse in the near distance as the birds chirp along atop a weather-worn fence nearby.

I needed these outside elements today, to *remember evermore* the gifts you and these horses both gave me, so many years ago. Needed to smell the fresh turn of manure, and to feel the gentle, sturdy earth beneath me—

the way dirt is so clean,

as my hands sit atop the fresh strands of grass.

When I was young, my father, in his medical perspective, said that I must choose between the movements needed for ballet or riding.

"You can't do both, you'll injure yourself." He felt the body's developing musculature could not accommodate the two contrasting forms of athleticism. I was given the opportunity to make my own inward decision.

And, at eight years old, knowing without knowing why, I drifted away from those cedar barres, and walked toward the dirt-infused grounds of the barn.

Little did I know in the realms of my mind that you and those horses would hold me on course through the crumbling times that would follow his death.

That together, you would teach me how to approach what felt too high to get over, and to find a way toward the base with steady, unwavering directness and to jump through my fears anyway. Even when feeling my own inner uncertainty try to deter me, through the air, I discovered I could still land upright on the other side. Until one day, the joy of soaring replaced the fear.

I did fall hard into the dirt—and was thrown, bucked off, kicked in the face, and fallen on.

But you showed me how to get back up—to get back on again, and do it right.

I had to learn to press forward and *continue*—even when my tears blurred the path in front of me, and my pride and body hurt.

We saw the course through. Worked through what wasn't working at all, until the time when we could end a lesson on a good note.

At four-fifteen in the morning, the alarm went off in the dark and cold guest room of your house, where I was huddled beneath layers of thin, wool, championship coolers I used as blankets. One of the other riders was asleep in the bed across from mine beneath the window that overlooked the large, Western-style upper-barn, and she rose instantly from her bed, shuffling her way to the bathroom with the first sound of the bell.

I reached my thin, long arm into the cool air outside the blanket, and pressed *snooze.*

When the light from the hallway entered the bedroom a few minutes later, I arose from the warm haven of sleep and fumbled for my clothing as she made her bed. My breeches, collared shirt, thin leather belt, and fleece jacket had all been laid out flatly the night before in anticipation for the early rise of dawn. Undressing in the chill of the room, zipping the sideline of my breeches and clasping them closed at the top, I layered myself beneath the same sweats I had slept in and my second-hand fleece, before pulling nude knee-highs over my calves, and loosely making my bed.

My sleepy fellow rider had already descended downstairs. I closed the bedroom door and walked down the creaking stairs toward the kitchen where she was sitting quietly on a barstool at the counter, and you stood awake beneath the light, a black cup of coffee in hand, ready to depart.

The kitchen in your house was warm in the dimmed lighting, and you were characteristically both stylishly and practically dressed for the day—hunter-green slacks, a thoughtful sweater, and straw hat akin to equestrians at the showgrounds. At eleven years old, I was an overtly thin, short-standing girl of five-feet—and you stood only slightly taller at five-foot-two, your red-blonde hair recently cut to resemble a well-known country singer of the time, its layers spiking to the sides of your face and down the back of your head where it was cut into a bob. Though you were the same age as my own parents, you had begun your family rearing earlier.

"Are you girls ready?" you said, setting your coffee into the sink and getting straight to the point. My friend and I simultaneously *mhmm'd,* knowing better than to offer any alternative that early in the morning.

The three of us walked out the front door and into the cold morning air that burst upon us as the screen door slammed shut and then the front door to your house was closed. Walking and shuffling out to the car, a small line of turquoise hovered in the early morning sky. I slid into the front seat, having ridden in the backseat the evening before, and heard the melody of an old Tricia Yearwood song begin to play as you turned the ignition.

I used to think I hated country music, but now I sang softly and melodically to the lyrics.

The sun slowly began filtering into the bright morning blue, and we rounded the back corners of country roads as the seats finally began to warm, and a second wave of tiredness began setting in.

"You have the hack today," you said, referring to the flat class I would have between my two over fences.

"I know," I replied, trying to reassure you of my preparations for the day to come.

When we arrived at the showgrounds, I stepped foot onto the wet, grassy ground and headed straight for the barn to lunge my pony outside in the cold. In the center of the ring, I released the lunge rope as she began encircling me, a trot slowly increasing into a canter that soon became a gallop that pulled hard against my grip. I slid the end of the lunge rope under my backside and leaned in to counter her weight with my own, as I clicked behind her hind legs and encouraged her to discharge extra energy before I was on her back and in the schooling ring.

I listened to her hooves as they dug into the sand ring, pebbles kicking up behind her, and watched as she circled 'round and 'round and beneath the light of morning rising higher, the warm air from her nostrils releasing snorts of breath into the morning chill. When she finally began to tire, she and I walked back to the barn, where I examined the precisely placed braids in her mane and tail and led her to the wash rack to hose the sand off her legs, before putting her blanket back on and placing her back in her stall.

With a calculated gap of time ahead of me, I walked hungrily over to the concession stand, open at six-thirty in the morning to accommodate the riders, and ordered a hot chocolate and an egg sandwich. I sipped the hot chocolate and it slightly burned the inside of my mouth, and I walked over to the show ring to study the courses on the board—estimating the strides between jumps as I furrowed my brows, whispered the courses in memory, and bit into my sandwich.

Finished with my food, with my hands crossed over my chest and prepared to recite my courses for the day to you before my rounds, I sighed and spun on the back of my boot heels and turned back toward the barn, throwing the empty remnants of my breakfast into the trash. Like my show clothes laid out in the morning, my show pad, saddle, breast plate, and bridal had all been cleaned the night before. I clipped my pony between the crossties of an empty grooming stall, and brushed her shampooed and conditioned coat clean, then stuffed cotton balls down into her ears to muffle any loud sounds that could spook her. Rubbing baby oil over her muzzle to make it shine, I bent down and wrapped cotton polo wraps around her four legs for the warmup, before scraping a hoof-pick through the Vs of her hooves, dusting off the dirt and hair on my sweatpants as I set her legs back down, one at a time.

I left on her tail wrap, protecting that intricate braid, to be removed at the back gate before the course, while I brushed away the remaining shavings from her thick, black tail.

Tacked up, I left her in the crossties and went into the tack room to change, where I slid from the warmth of my sweats and fleece, and felt a new layer of cold air brush against my breeches. Grabbing the moist leather bridal from the hook and throwing it over my shoulder, I walked to my tack trunk, threw my clothes inside and picked up my boot pulls, before latching them onto the insides of my boots and pulling them over my legs, buffing them one more time. A blonde hairnet slid over my hair and ears, and tying my hair into a low ponytail, I flipped my snug helmet on from the back to the front of my head. Then I slid my arms through my dark navy show coat, buttoned the jacket, and tied my show number around my waist, closed the tack trunk, and headed back to the grooming stall with the chinstrap from my helmet dangling.

That pony stood sleepy-eyed, and I removed her halter, inserted my thumb to the side of her mouth, and felt the wet of her tongue as she opened her teeth and took in the bit from the bridal. The sound of metal grinding beneath round teeth chewed its way into the air as I slid the bridal over the poll of her head and behind her ears. Walking out of the crossties, I heard the clinking of her hooves on the cement, and stopping to place the reins on the saddle, I lifted my right leg into a ninety-degree bend and counted "one, two, three!"—as one of the grooms hoisted me into the air and onto the saddle.

"Thank you!" I said happily, as I slid my feet through the stirrups, and felt the rolling back-and-forth movement of the pony's body beneath me while we walked away from the barn toward the schooling ring.

After a focused warmup and a few schooling jumps, you and I walked together toward the back gate to review the course. A groom removed the tail and polo wraps and painted my pony's hooves black with oil that dripped thickly onto the ground. The echo of the emcee over the mic confirmed my name second at the gate, as we confirmed the course I had studied earlier in the morning.

"Down the single, up the six, down the seven, up the single oxer, and down the in-and-out. A four to a three to a two." I pointed to each fence as I spoke, demonstrating my preparation the way you had trained me to.

"Good," you said, following my gaze the entire time. "Make sure you get her to change her lead before the corner. Good luck."

Then you stood at the back gate as I walked into the show ring, and began trotting across the center to the opposite end of the ring to begin my round.

One of the most important lessons that crafted my sportsmanship happened that year, one morning after a poor round. I'd come in short, chipping two of the fences, and then botched the others by taking them too long. The failure of the round was extremely noticeable, and I received a score of a 68/100.

While I was still inside the ring, I collapsed the upper half of my body in transparent defeat, hunching my shoulders in failure as I moped my way out of the ring . . .

Rather than remain by the back gate to review my course, that day you took the reins and led me behind the arena, away from the other riders, trainers, and spectators, and even before you spoke, I could feel that you were mad.

"Don't *ever* come out of a round like that again. I don't care what happened . . . you never hunch over and make a face like that in the show ring!"

A pain-stricken shame filled my insides, and bore into my face, as I fell further into my humiliation with tears filling the brims of my eyes. You left me there alone that day, behind the arena, to stand in my failure.

Tears poured down my cheeks as I slinked back to the barn, where I hid in between the walls of the stalls and didn't emerge again for hours after my visible exposure and display of disappointment.

But I never collapsed that way again on the exterior, in or out of the ring—and later, won a sportsmanship award for riders eighteen and under.

Through Pacific Northwest winters that hardened the arena floors with crystals of ice spreading prisms throughout dirt that numbed the tips of my toes, to Canadian rains that slicked the damp fields of grass, and hot, dehydrating, dry days of summer of the desert that hovered over a hundred degrees and plummeted to near freezing temperatures at night as my teeth chattered from inside a bundled tent—

every season of riding held its own demands.

During the shows, grooms ran to help late, anxious riders to tack up their horses, while trainers walked prestigiously toward the rings, and riders who had completed their courses sat half-dressed and gossiping among each other at the end of the day. Hooves thumped rhythmically upon hard grounds, while sand in jumper rings slammed against fences, followed by moments of ascended silence in the air as horse and rider flew, landing on the other side of jumps—and I grew a deep love of those familiar glimpses of time, when I was a kid being a kid, on the minimal and short grasses of youth.

I set free bursts of jocular play—as I galloped beneath vast setting skies, standing high in my saddle and swinging my arms overhead like a cowboy lassoing through iridescent pink-orange clouds, and choreographed musical skits from behind the collection of motor homes to be performed at the end of the day. A boisterous laugh would sound out when you'd say, "You're such a ham"—and the truth was that I was.

Honest, youthful moments ensued in greater ease through these years when I was with you, between my barn and home life, with its crumbling bouts of collapse and jarring "catastrophes." A mom of one of the other riders soon offered to pick me up from my junior high roundabout and drive me to the barn, and I would run down the aisles, gaily shouting your name, before jumping into your arms to greet you. I slept over at your house on Friday nights between the shows, in part to work off some of my board and mostly so I could still ride on Saturdays, as I scooped cold grains into tin buckets and stirred them with herbs, oil, and vinegar, the horses whinnying with early morning anticipation of their individualized daily remedies.

I cleaned hanging girths over the saddle bar with Murphy Oil and soap and water, and the smell of horsehair and damp leather creased together next to the thick, warm sweat of woven Mexican saddle pads, whose small, imbedded remnant horse hairs stuck to my hands as I dropped them into the laundry. My chaps made my jeans crease and stick to my legs after those eight hour days, and I felt relief in my muscles and soul when I unzipped them down the side of my leg, and threw them over the rail in the grooming stall in the evening.

Amid all the work and play and growing pains, I had a steadfast feeling when I finished all of my tasks at the end of the day, that I had a place where I belonged, and in my spirit,

> I could still feel that I was accomplishing something
> meaningful.

A feeling arising deep from the ground in those dependable rhythms reverberated throughout that season of life, in years that spanned falls and winters, and numerous springs and summers.

∽

For the two years my dad fought dying, and in those that followed his death when I was thirteen, my mom turned a new side of herself front-forward while she fell into and then apart within the arms of her new boyfriend. In between the riding and training, in the quieter moments of space between work, you and I had moments together, where I could air with honesty the circumstances of life at home. I could say to you, then:

"They're drinking again"—

"They fought so loud the neighbors heard—"

And, "I think my brother is getting high . . ."

You would look down, leaning on the marble kitchen counter between us, and behind you I could see through the window above the sink the sturdy presence of the barn in the distance— quiet and large and reassuring.

You weren't deterred by what I brought to you. You matched my unfolding story with reflection and insight, and with both compassion and empathy, you refrained mostly from judgement toward my family.

You had seen your own rough days.

But when you talked with me, you opened a place for me to step into, where acknowledgment offered me what I so desperately needed in some other adult to organize my experience and to be seen and known.

You gave me an arena to portray the real-lived life of youth existing beneath my youthlike appearance.

Burdensome worlds on thin-framed shoulders, and the neglect that came from so many people missing what they simply chose not to see.

To be honest with you was for me to be real, and to be less alone in the reality of what was.

After talking, I would wander to the upper barn and sit on a haystack overlooking the fields and your house. Thankful for the aroma of sweet-smelling, dry hay.

When I look back now, it must have been something to contend with—the life you saw unfold, year after year, and what both I and my circumstances asked of you. My mother competing with me on the showgrounds, as she took up riding herself, and forsook my needs to attend to her own, while I looked to you to fill the gap. The way when my dad was dying, I would ask every few weeks, "How long do you think he has to live?"—and hope you could divine the answer no one could predict.

I showed up to the barn with no food for lunch in those years— large appetite amid my abnormally thin frame. Metaphors of the orphaned, full of sneezing and coughing allergies, youthful enthusiasm and uncertainty, living life's brute force on my emotionally transparent sleeve, limping in pain from a sore back, and tensing and crying, uncertain of where there was a need to brace.

"Put your shoulders down," you said, over and over again, as I cantered in circles around you.

It wasn't just a season, short-lived and passing—but one that endured, for years that stacked on top of the other.

When my family filed for bankruptcy, I wore another wealthier rider's boots, half a size too big, and tripped down the aisles—

and found I was still somehow able to continue riding, even though I was sure we could no longer afford it, and my weekend work at the barn would never cover the cost . . .

You had a steadfastness, and durability—
to stay beside people. And not just let them go.
Faithfulness and loyalty to stay the course.
Even when caring can become a burden we're unsure of how to love.

The horses were their own brand of companionship, a healing balm to soothe a wounded soul. But even they could become a source of anxiety from time to time. Their largeness, and their power.

All of those falls.

Thrown from the saddle and slammed into jumps and walls. Kicked in the head by jerking hooves, bucked off in the dead of winter and thudding, *hard*, onto the frozen ground. In the year before I turned twelve, my pony slipped on the grass in the rain, and fell on top of me, as my helmet came unbuckled and rolled away from my head. I awoke in bits of unconsciousness meeting consciousness, head-swollen throbbing that came in and out, and felt your frustration, when I told you in the days to come that I still didn't feel right, after that grade three concussion.

There is an impact from being responsible for another person's child through injuries that can take a severe toll. I couldn't tell then whether it was care or sincere irritation—when your anger came through.

I absorbed the shame from the undertones in your voice, for not being able to *think* my way into feeling better, *being better.*

These were the interplays that were built from our circumstances, and the way our own limitations crashed against each other, in responses we sometimes only short-handedly embark, just by living through what perhaps none of us should have to bear.

You yelled at me from across grass fields in the scorching summer heat, the way trainers often do, angry and exasperated. My capacity to fire on all cylinders dwindled upon the backs of ponies I could not get to halt or change leads, as I yanked and pulled to no avail, and severed temporarily beneath my uncontrollable tears and fraying nerves.

Helplessness in feeling is perhaps felt on both ends, and they collided together as we did: your yelling, and my hyperventilating tears. The midday sun blazing down upon my black velvet helmet and fourteen-year-old brain. Lightheaded, fuzzy. No strength left to pull, no ability left to halt, blood sugar plummeting. My body no longer functioning with the alignment of my intentions, no matter how much I *pulled and pulled*, and *leaned*, or *tried*.

And the tears that poured and poured and poured, as your voice echoed yelling across the vast open fields in the summer air.

But by midafternoon, we were always friends again.

I emerged from the stables after a lonely cry by the stalls, or an exhausted nap in the humid holding of a quiet tent by the motor homes, and went out to find you—schooling the older riders for their afternoon rounds. I looked left and right between rhythms of cantering hooves as if crossing some invisible grass-worn line, and walked to the other side of a jump where you were standing, intuiting the time to raise the height and asked, "one post or two?"—and we raised the opposite sides one latch, finding our way back into harmony together.

You concentrated your gaze on the older riders, which I followed with the focus of my own, and you later said: "We're always friends again by the afternoon, aren't we?" as we walked side by side back to the barn away from the show ring. My eyes rose up to look at you smiling, responding—"Yeah"—gladly, and in agreement.

Relief followed that semblance of repair, which I could not know within the fringes of so much of the rest of my life.

You were sturdy and nurturing—and you could be sparing with your praise.

One sunny day back at the barn, in the lazy afternoon hours that spanned between the shows in the summer, another of the trainers relayed echoes that you'd said *I was good.*

The surprise shimmered through my mind and widening eyes, dropping and circulating through my receptive and desperate body—as I responded to the struggle I carried in trying to believe what might be true in the absence of what was spoken. So when she said, "You ride well because you *feel* instead of having to be *told,*" I was centered by your peripheral words that lent some resonating joy toward the developing understanding I was making of myself.

You never told me yourself. But hearing these words, even from someone else, filled me with a glowing, quiet anchoring and pride, as I didn't suppress the smile on my face, and the back of my legs began to numb from the metal fence where I was sitting, another rider circling by, the trainer saying, "Don't pull on the reigns so much, give him some room," from beside me.

∾

You were the first real spiritual presence in my life. So much of what you gave me has remained with me through the years, the way true lessons do.

I suspect you came into my life when I needed you most—
and that the shift within me to finally move away took place in
the time when it was right for me to begin letting go.

Like all things, I suppose we remain together for the time we
are meant to.

Every season eventually ends.

But saying goodbye without helping each other can make letting go hard—and in truth, more like severing than a natural
leaving.

I think this happens when people are silent in their good-
byes . . .

The journey of progressing from the small backs of ponies to my
own horse had been a long one, and gave me a course to stay to
through those years. By the time I was fifteen, I'd had Patrick for
a year—and I'd grown from initial hesitation to love that wrapped
through my arms in an embrace around his large, long neck, as I
smelled his soft, sweet hair.

His canter rolled long beneath my own lengthening limbs;
slow and large in stride, he never threw me to the ground. He was
beautiful, just as much as he was kind.

Even amid the cultivation of something good, sometimes a
body of knowing can begin to exist inside—a message that the
time has come for us to go. Something essential begins to plague
until we are ready to acknowledge its existence fully—the way I
felt that knowing as a lump of truth within the bottom of my
stomach.

At first a thought that I disregarded, and then a resonant
knowing in the pit of my soul—I began budding toward other
possibilities and experiences in my young life.

But I knew, with the decision to quit riding, that I would be changed . . .

When it was finally time to say the words aloud, it was late on a Tuesday afternoon at the end of summer, my first year of high school just around the bend. I sat in your back office where the windows were open, and through them, the breezes of change moved with trepidation and invitation—as my mouth trembled and tears bequeathed my eyes, and I said words I had once never believed would come.

I wouldn't look at you at first, and kept my gaze down on the mahogany table in front of me, away from your absorbent attention. Until finally, after a moment of silence, you said, "I'll cry about this later, when I'm at home . . ."

I looked up at you, surprise meeting deep-felt relief—

because tears from you felt like something of love.

Once it had been said, I guess there wasn't much to do but let the life we had lived dissolve.

I finished the tail end of that show season, and felt what I'd sensed with other riders before—a silent shift of subtle movement out of your circle that always seemed to come with goodbye, and often took place even before people began to leave.

Something deep inside of me hoped, and perhaps concretely believed, that goodbye between us wouldn't really happen at all. The truth is, I didn't know what real ending was, and so the longing I hoped for, became what I expected—

that your presence in my life would never really leave.

On the day I heard my footsteps echo down the barn aisle for the last time, no one was there to say anything. And in the silence of the aisles, during the dipping hours of late afternoon, I stood in heaviness, rather than delightful anticipation.

I looked over the quiet aisles toward the stalls, tracing the memories all the years of bustling movement had given me.

My eye caught the empty door of the stall where I knew Patrick stood inside—all sixteen hands,

> with a sore back like mine,

> and a tongue that dangled to make me laugh from beneath my tears.

When he'd let me lie with him down in the warmth of the shavings of his stall, he had been a large presence of unconditional love—

and so had you . . .

And like the absence of goodbye you gave to me, I wasn't able to find my way to a goodbye with him, either.

I stood there, in the center of that aisle, for a moment I both did and did not want to pass—

> before walking away, crying in heaviness and shame,

> as I left him alone in that stall,

> and never called his name again.

One year later, sixteen and now able to drive wherever I pleased, I found I could no longer escape the need for the smell of hay, manure, shavings, and horses.

The tires of my car began to crunch over gravel, and I opened my window to hear the announcer on the overhead, an excited, familiar sense of having found my way back arose at the grounds of a nearby show. I parked, and heard voices of trainers yelling, the sounds of clucking riders, and sand kicked from within the rings, and I made my way toward the familiarity of the showgrounds.

A low churn of anxiety laced with excitement leapt in my stomach at the thought of reunion, as I smiled and skipped a step or two before settling into a full-paced stride looking for you.

Out across an arena there was a rider on course, and to the left, the stables with their rows of stalls and signature barn colors. Spectators crossed back-and-forth, golf carts stood parked on the side rings, and on the silver shining metal stands, riders sat watching each other.

After stepping around some horses and patting their large bodies from behind, I saw you, standing next to the warm-up ring.

"Don't let him get away from you like that . . ."

Your voice was the same as I remembered.

The clanking of horseshoes upon the pavement clapped rhythmically, and I walked up beside you in silence, crossing my arms with my focus straight ahead, watching the rider being schooled.

I pressed my lips together to keep from smiling, and when you finally registered that someone was beside you, you glanced over and grinned widely, laughing aloud with joy. "You sneaky girl! What are you doing here?!"

I broke my smile, delighted by my surprise, and turned, hugging you and laughing, so glad to be beside you again . . .

I hung around for a little while that day, alongside familiar faces and recognizing smiles, and for a moment felt a comfort arise within the reliability of the changelessness of that place—a small arena of life where the horses, people, sounds, and smells stay pretty much the same. And although the sameness was a balm easing a subtle ache developed in the passing of time—I knew, also, that things were different.

As the hours moved along that day, I discovered what was once my innate sense of timing within that world, of what to do and where to be, had begun to dissipate. And I realized the navigation I had once used through all of those peculiar, changing rhythms of the day was gone.

I returned to an acknowledgment of what I already knew—

that I was out of place, in a world no longer mine.

That though I had once belonged, I now no longer did.

I ended the day and drove home, a sense of loss amid a newly growing sensation I was also beginning to acknowledge for the first time in my young life—

that when we leave something, we really do *leave.*

Today, I smell manure from that pasture nearby, as I walk to the fence and lean over the post, listening to the occasional snort of a large presence, and wonder if I regret my decision to leave the barn so many years ago.

As I remember with longing, the rhythms that came from simply being in motion with another animal, and from standing through so many seasons with you by my side.

We can't see the fullness of what we may be letting go of in the moments we walk away. The shapes of what we leave are so much more than what we can perceive in our small views at the time, their layers so much more full-bodied than what we can imagine. In the loss of what we let go, the structures of life shift, and whatever we have left creates open ground where something can arise into our lives anew.

Even when I yearn to feel the warmth of his breath upon my hand, and the freedom of rising in the air, as my legs grip a large body beneath me, rounding over the arch of one of those jumps—I know that to feel both *the grief of loss* and *the familiar comfort of my memories* is what holding true to what has been and healing really is . . .

I drive somewhere far away along acres of farm fields, with rolling grasses of hay, the smell of sweet and familiar earth blowing through my open windows, as a country song plays on the radio, and then, finally returning home, I pause on the gravel outside my door and wonder—

how many times do we circle through the past and then come back?

Remedies from the medicine we are given hold a healing link, when we take old lessons and apply them to the ground of today—in the remembrance, without the return.

I pause when I remember you. And your life still lingers, and ripples within mine.

And I know: *That I have grown because of the presence you gave me.*

The way that you impart each of those whom you touch, with a brief bit of magic that is only yours.

What then, can I regret?

The breeze where I sit settles over me, and I let go of my need to consider the possibilities of what might have been had I decided to stay.

Because I trust the course we took together—and can let that meaning rest where it lay.

Sitting on the hard ground in the grass of a field in the early evening, the sun becomes a deeper gold with each passing minute, and the warmth of day still lingers faithfully as the smell of summer and earth surround me.

I hold a piece of uncut grass between my fingers, and a horse's tail swishes swiftly somewhere nearby, as the step of a hoof upon the ground reminds me with subtle gesture that I am not alone.

And I remember to let my shoulders down.

Saturdays

— Mom —

You told me that when I was young and breastfeeding, I bit your nipples.

I wondered about the legitimacy of the story, knowing the discrepancy sometimes between your take on things and mine.

But then, I could also sense the truth in it, maybe even the likelihood—since I know the distaste I've experienced toward much of what you have tried to feed me through the years. The sour discarding from which I've had to wean . . .

I suppose my palate could not conform, even from the earliest beginning of my life—to the acrid contrast between rich but miniscule nutrients, lack, and intrusiveness—

> within a moment, within a room, or within our relationship.

Truth is, I think I would bite at that.

And gnaw, with scared and devastated eyes, not knowing what else to do.

I am still confronting this oscillation for what it is. And I still reach sometimes, for what I know will not be there.

They are brief, and uninvested longings.

We lived tucked into the woods at the end of a small dirt road for a period of our childhood, in a house Dad designed behind the hidden, closed doors of his office in the quiet hours of night, after long days at work.

I remember the way my bedroom windows faced the tall, green, closely gathered evergreens just outside, and the way the trees comforted me. In the changes that took place through the hours of the day, I could see the light's many angles alter their presence, as different shadows floated across the floor of my room. And the enormity of their darkened silhouettes outside my window, drifting in the wind against the deep, black, night sky.

When I was eleven, I came home one fall afternoon to find you had changed my room . . .

In the place of the small white daybed that for years had been my sleepy landing, stood a large queen-sized sleigh bed, warm with cherrywood paneling. An old antique dresser was placed newly beside the bed, wise and enchanting with worn crevices— and the wood between the two pieces played between each other, both accenting and differing from the other.

At the corner edge of the bed, a woven straw hat with a soft pink ribbon sat on top of the comforter—as if the room were within the layout of a magazine. And across the room, a pillow, tilted ever so slightly on the window seat beneath my tree-loving window.

A small, dim-lit lamp sat atop the dresser casting a warm glow . . .

As I walked into the room beneath the sinking light of early evening, everything felt warm. You had arranged flowers on the dresser next to the bed, placing them thoughtfully, their pale, warm colors and deep green leaves bunched within a clean and clear vase of water.

"Mom!!!" I said excitedly.

"Do you like your room?"

You had a gentle settledness in your voice, flush with a creative sort of pride, soft with excited anticipation to share what you had done.

It felt like the warmth of mothering—

of love.

When I was a girl, we often sailed in the San Juans—you, Dad, Toey, and I.

Out near Sucia Island one night, we prepared to depart from our sleepy anchor to another island nearby in the dusk of the horizon on our dinghy "the meter boat."

I never knew how you came up with your nicknames for things.

That night, no one else was tucked into the small harbor except two quiet boats buoyed next to ours that slank silently in the gentle waters. Standing at the stern of the sailboat, I looked down into the dinghy as you revved up the engine, and the water stirred the dark, cold blue, blades cutting a current of swirling circular motion. Toey and I held hands to steady each other, and stepped in, feeling the weight of our bodies press the small boat farther into the water, as it made a gentle splashing sound against the large, ascending side of the sailboat.

The cold off the Puget Sound surrounded us in the air as we sat in a descended place, both within and above the water. Finally, Dad stepped on, the boat sunk farther again, and untying the thin lines from around the cleat that connected us to our temporary home, he pushed us away from the warm enclave of our boat, as you lightly accelerated, taking us farther toward an empty horizon.

We passed the tip of the island in floating motion, its hard rock cliffs reaching jaggedly toward the open waters, and the earth was reflected in a smooth, flat mirror upon the surface of the Sound, as you drove the boat from the dark shadowing harbor out onto the stretching blue, the pink of the sun sinking beneath a luminous darkening blue sky.

The water's surface, glasslike, opened upon a grand scape of ocean, and so too did the world grow slowly darker, and cooler, as we headed farther away from the comfort of our harbor fading out of view.

You caught glimpse of some ducks out on the bay, and in an instant, I was gripping the handles of the dinghy, enthralled with excitement and subtle fear as you sped up toward maximum thrust to chase the flapping fowl from their free-floating serenity in the dusk. With each turn of the engine handle, each rev, the front of the dinghy tipped farther up, and the back end sunk into the churning water, as you sped loudly, the engine roaring beneath the muffled undertow into the silent waters of the untouched night.

"Hey, you guys! Get up front to hold us down!" you yelled into the chilly air.

Toey and I crawled carefully from the center of the little din-ghy toward the bow, tucked beneath our thick, polyvinyl life jackets that rubbed our faces with billowing shoulders lifting to-ward our ears.

"Whoo-hoo!" you yelled from behind.

I looked back from the tip of the dinghy, wind blowing tiny hair strands against my face into my wet, watering eyes, and I saw you seated on the bench at the stern, beer tucked inside a nautical grip, as you looked out wondrously over the night. Turning forward to face the open waters, feeling the wind biting against my skin, making its way through the neck of my sweatshirt, I looked over the side of the dinghy at the gap between the still, flat ocean water and the underside of the boat. We moved with biting speed, and the water was so silent—like we weren't floating but glazing above, the glass-like surface blazing beneath the weight of the rubber bottom breaking through the stillness of it all.

We zigged and zagged in large, tilting circles as you chased the ducks, flapping wet, heavily watered wings in their attempts to escape, and I could hear the tiny chattering teeth of excitement gurgling up as a giggle or two from Toey beside me. My face was beginning to numb, and the flying sensation within my stomach began to make me nauseous. Dad sat next to you, and I caught his voice, muffled through the wind, as he said "Alright, not too fast," and you sighed with unfiltered annoyance, the roaring buzz of the engine dropping abruptly to a muffled churning, and the boat leveled itself flatly back on top of the water, and we headed in a deflated, straight, slow line toward the edge of the beach.

When we were pulled up onto the shore, the dinghy tied loosely to the large smooth end of a piece of beachfront driftwood, we gathered around the pit of a fire and you ventured briefly away and out of sight while Dad lit the flames.

A moment later, returning, you held a small, slightly twisted stick, smoothed by the waves, a dozen miniature-like rivers trickling in curvature over the wood.

The sky was slipping farther into night, but the world was not yet fully dark. We sat together as a family—on a couple of long beach logs, rolling forward and back with each shift of another's body, smiling and laughing as the fire crackled, and when a small pothole of air burst inside one of the logs, the wood resettled itself atop the cool, cold sand. Seaweed, dried and darkened green, was scattered, paper-thin all over the beach, on top of small rocks pebbled together toward the shore. And not far away, was the slight sound of small, gentle waves lapping at the water's edge.

The night was cold despite Dad's fire, and I hugged myself to find greater warmth inside. When I looked at you across from me, I saw that you were in a wavelength of consuming thought.

I waited into the quiet as a plume of smoke blew in and around me, causing my eyes to water into the change of air.

"We're going to do something called 'Pass the Stick,'" you said, then paused . . .

"I want each of us to share something that's been upsetting them. When it's your turn, you will hold the stick, and tell us as a family what's been on your mind."

My eyes widened slightly with curious intrigue, and looking up to the sky, a subtle sense of excitement arose from within my stomach and began to tingle, telling me I liked this game, as I pondered through an inventory of what to share.

Across from me, I could feel the underlying discomfort in Dad, as he cleared his throat and shifted on the log.

Toey sat quiet beside me.

"Who wants to go first?" you asked.

After everyone had shared, reluctantly and openly, and a spark of firewood had flown into Toey's eye, causing him to scream and cry, we walked back down to the lapping shore and all stood witness—as Dad wrapped something around the end of a large piece of wood, and lit the wood on fire.

He held the burning flame, and his voice quivered through a trembled crying.

"This one's for you, Pa," he whispered, and the stick flamed before the now black, star-speckled sky.

Both of our grandpas, Pa and Papa, had just died, only six months apart.

Dad threw the flame far off the shore, and I watched it sink and disappear into the heavy waters below.

When I was little and frustrated, you used to ask me, "Do you need to go beat up a pillow?"

You used to say, "Crying is very healthy, Christina. It's good to get out what is upsetting you."

These are the ingredients I remember of you growing up, those that nourished me—

> when you could intuit the needs of others, and
> > encouraged us all to bring forward what was inside,
> from behind the walls of a façade,
> with emotional openness and honesty.

There were pictures of you dispersed around the house, framed on the walls. Modeling photos. Hanging, they gazed down in black-and-white hues over soft, ivory country wallpaper.

I kept the discarded remnants of your portfolio in the closet of my bedroom, with its pictures, flyers, and cutouts of magazines strewn incongruently inside the old, dark leather case. The zipper was thick and often stuck around the wide handles that I tried to unzip when I wanted to uncover the pictures of you from when you were young.

I think I looked trying to find myself in your face . . .

When I gazed at those pictures often as a young girl, I found I was drawn to those where you were natural, smiling, not wearing much makeup—as laughter on your face erupted youthfully and with uncontoured joy.

I preferred the natural photos to the ones that were sharp and serious; where makeup covered the bare face I knew from behind closed doors, and your looks were intense, and with a cutting edge.

One afternoon, when I was twelve, you said to me while sitting in the living room, "The designers all loved my legs . . . it's because I'm so tall, and my legs are so long and thin."

You paused and drew the burning, ashy smoke of a cigarette into the back of your throat while you sat gazing out the window.

Silence hovered in the smoke-filling air, and I widened my eyes to hear more of the truth-telling that was coming.

"You don't have my legs," you said, as you flicked the cigarette and looked outside. "You're going to be hippy."

I listened, and looked over at the floor, as you shook your head in disappointment.

"It's a shame you didn't get my legs . . ." you said.

You and Dad liked to entertain, in a laid-back, loose, but elegant environment, where Dad cooked gourmet meals and everyone drank fine wine.

Friends became regular extensions of our family, and I used to love to come into the room where you were gathered—for hugs and hellos, to sit on the laps of others, and to listen and partake in the adult conversations.

One evening, I came excitedly downstairs, running and skipping into the living room, music playing and voices chattering, and made my way around the circle of guests, wrapping my arms around waists as I said *hi* and gave updates on my happenings at school.

Still circulating amidst the small crowd, I heard you loudly whisper my name from the corner of the room.

"Christina!"

I turned my head to you and raised my eyes in question, smiling. "Yeah?" I said back.

"You look ridiculous," you said. "Go put something else on—" and you flicked your hand at me disgustedly toward the top of the stairs.

Your friends began to catch on to the change in tune, and heads slowly turned, eyes peering into me, people looking me over, up and down, as a new tone slowly took the room in its grasp.

My eyes darted away but didn't know where to look, as I glanced down over myself and tried to understand but couldn't— because I was wearing something you'd just bought me for Christmas. When I looked back to you in confusion, you rolled your eyes, as if embarrassed.

One or two people smiled at me with a dipped sort of sympathy.

I shook myself from the hold of the room and rushed upstairs to hide for the rest of the evening.

But no one ever said a thing.

It was by that time, when I was reaching early adolescence, that I was beginning to sense if I stayed too near to you, something inside of me would be trampled.

The definition of *flourish* is "to grow luxuriously" and "to thrive."

Alongside the thinning crumbs of your nurturance, thorns and weeds worked harder to take me down, and to damage me in my roots.

The opposite of flourishing is "to die," or "to wither."

When Dad died in early November 1998, I was in eighth grade, and you sat in your nightgown, legs crossed, smoking cigarettes and sipping white wine on the floor in front of the fire in the living room.

Every day, when I came home from school, that's where you'd be: seated, in front of the fireplace. Wearing that thin, overly short white nightgown with small, light pink flowers on it. Rocking gently back-and-forth . . .

Then, blaring tunes of *David Gray* would sound through the downstairs of the house later in the night as you broke the silence, and danced with Toey and me to the repeating *Babylon* song with the lights shining bright.

One night, I cleaned your vomit off the floor, warm and thick, putrid with tanging traces of white chardonnay and macaroni and cheese. Swiping it clean with an old towel, I poured hot water over the carpet to scrub it away. Beside me, you were in tears, sobbing, gasping, and sweating.

"I'm so sorry, I'm so sorry," you said, as you sobbed.

It was painful—seeing you in that much pain.

But it hurt even more to feel it from beside you in the room . . .

Shame and travesty have a porousness to their emissions.

The truth is, I'm not sure how much I minded the cleaning; recently, your comparisons of me to Dad, his capabilities and sense of responsibility, echoed proudly in my mind. I felt strong to discover a calm in the face of that chaos, to discover it was enough to help me handle what was falling around me. I felt good—discovering I somehow instinctively knew what to do in order to take care of our house and the people in it: paying the bills with a friend, asking you to sign the checks, turning out the lights, and asking Toey if he'd had any dinner.

"I'm so proud of you. You're just like your father," you'd say . . .

I heard your words echo in my mind as I scrubbed the floor.

When I finished cleaning the vomit, I placed my hand gently on the heat of your back, rubbing it softly.

"It's okay, Marmee."

You sobbed and gasped through gut-deep, choking tears. "No, it's not . . ." you said.

I was thirteen years old.

It started before he died. But in the time that followed, the emotional outbursts became worse.

Often, it was during a holiday dinner, when something unprovoked and yet seemingly unavoidable would erupt from you. An emotional, tearful outpouring would follow some wound no one could clearly see.

I knew from an early age about the struggles you lived through in your youth, and what you yourself had *survived,* and a heart-heavy compassion often intertwined with incomprehension in those moments of downward spiraling. Rarely were there any logical ties to connect the dots between even-keeledness and emotional overwhelm, though like a sixth sense, I could often feel them coming.

And just as the tide was turning, I'd look over at Toey—
    and we'd set down our forks, almost synchronously,
    as the sound of our kitchen chairs slid over the floor
        from either side of the table and we stood,
    walking to either side of you,
        to hug you,
    as your head sat within your hands.
"It's okay Mommy, don't be sad," we'd say, and rub your arms and back. "We love you."

Rapid, shallow, heaving gulps of air, like hiccupping tears would erupt as you tried to breathe between raw sobs. We stood there, trying to comfort you . . . but were never able to fully understand what had brought upon the ill perceptions of our intentions— that fed in you an over-reactivity,
    in a vulnerability that went deeper than mere sensitivity,
    somewhere nearer the realms of collapse.

But seeing you crumble like that, *so easily*, with so much hurt inside, all coming out at once—hurt to watch.

And it hurt to feel from beside you.

Two months after Dad died, you met a man in the mountains in January when your Tahoe got stuck in the snow. You were four-wheeling with Toey and a teen you'd befriended after working a brief period as a volunteer in a school for disruptive students.

The next evening, when you invited the man over to the house, before he arrived, you asked Toey and me if we minded you seeing someone.

Truth is I was glad at first—to have someone else enter the picture. Someone to give you something of what you might need. I pushed any of my own needs aside, without really acknowledging them in the first place. The tug to attend to your deprivations was always more strongly felt, or perhaps easily attended to, than the devastation I was unable to fully register with regard to the gnawing absences in my own lived experience. I turned away from the pain of that neglect, and attended to what was more readily available and expected of me: taking care of you.

The man was tall and large with brown hair, bright blue eyes, and a mustache. He drove a red Chevy truck that roared steadily as it came and went from the driveway. The cadence of that coming and going became a benchmark of the years that followed— for the hold placed on you and our house, marked by the reverberating sound of that engine.

The house had degraded during Dad's dying, and inside the walls of the country charm, dry layers of dust and animal hair lay atop expensive pieces of furniture—cream-colored couches turning a dim, faded putrid brown, and dirt was crammed within the lining of our glass-covered coffee table with beech wood paneling. Your wine bottles had been a steady presence for a while, but with the arrival of your new companion, now had their own counterpart in empty bottles of beer, which sourly stained the insides of our overflowing recycling bins I had to take up the driveway weekly, as the loud, shocking sounds of empty anesthetics hit the curb and rolled down the concrete while I inched one leg at a time beneath the weight of clanking glass.

Where you had previously been struggling day-to-day in heapfull collapses on the floor by the fire, now your presence became obscure, and you often disappeared altogether.

Behind your locked bedroom door in the middle of the day, you'd yell at me for "interrupting you" as I tried to deliver phone calls from the friends you now ignored—and you vanished for long hours into the night, without ever letting Toey and I know where you were.

I started to become subtly panicked as the day dipped into the night, and you ignored my phone calls to figure out where you were at 5:30 p.m., 7:00 p.m., 9:10 p.m., 9:55 p.m., and 11:30 p.m. on school nights . . .

Finally, I'd hear a lift of the receiver on the other end of the line. "God, what?! What do you want??"

"I just wanted to know where you were, Mom. It's really late?"

"Leave me alone! I'll be home later . . ." And you'd hang up the phone.

When you were at home, you were with him, and the two of you hung around, lounging through the middle of the day, giddy, obsessive, and "in love."

I suppose it was better than you throwing-up or rocking, alone, on the floor.

Interspersed between too much or too little presence, I often came home to a locked door after school because you'd forgotten to leave it open for me when you'd left the house.

I crawled through the cat door on the side of the house to get inside.

You married that man later that year, and he became our stepdad. The years passed, and fluctuations between obsessive clinging and outbursts of fighting ensued.

In some ways, I was used to the rhythm of chaotic conflict. Before Dad died, you both had begun to fight in such a way that my system ignited into sudden forms of reactive alarm.

Now, in place of where I had once dashed in front of you while you and Dad screamed at each other, I was doing the same with your "soulmate."

Fights took place at all hours of the day, but when they came late at night, I would tiptoe to my bedroom door to listen for the pitch of voices—raising, *not too loud*—as I discerned whether to intervene. The floor would creak from the door next to mine, and it would softly open, as Toey peered through and we'd look at each other, waiting to see what to do next.

Inside, I oscillated between fear and anger. Moments before, I'd been settled in the peace of sleep—my backpack packed and ready for school, homework done, clothes laid out on the chair. I'd been listening to quiet evening music, everything clean, with the window open and a breeze streaming into my bedroom upstairs—

now, I was rushing down the stairs, lightning-quick, bursting in front of you, and yelling at our stepdad, telling him—

"GET AWAY FROM MY MOM!"

I was the tiniest teenager before I hit puberty. But protective rage inside outweighed any logical hesitation for me to intervene.

"Soul Mate" would stand in front of me for a moment, and stare at me.

Then, scoff and walk out the door.

Of course, after the dust had settled, you would turn and yell at me for making him leave . . .

For years, after the fighting ended, with the sound of that engine roaring up the street as that large red truck sped away, I watched you sit on the edge of a chair in the living room—staring out the window, waiting for him to return.

For hours, you sat and waited. Sometimes, you picked at your legs until they bled, and scabs began to form, which were then torn away again before they could heal. And then one night, I found you in the bathroom, painting purple makeup over a single eye to make it look bruised.

"Shut up, Christina," you said to me, exposed in a scheme you didn't want revealed.

Then, just as always, he would come back.

You would rush to greet him, with desperate, whining love, and then you would cling to each other, as the two of you made up, and then the next morning, acted as if nothing had happened.

Walking down the bottom of the stairs, I'd see you both smiling from the sunshine pouring into the kitchen.

"Hi, Anna! How are you?!"

I scrunched my eyes, looked sideways, and cocked my head.

Then you'd both roll your eyes. "Oh God, here she goes again."

"Everything's fine, Christina. We're fine, okay?"

"Get over it."

I shook my head and sighed, rolling my eyes, as I condensed my anger into a silent inward armor and went to make tea at the sink.

An irony developed in all the years between those outbursts, between you and Dad, and you and our stepdad—

the one where I felt that I had to protect you.

The truth of it was, I think I had begun to sense that it was easier for me to have my back turned toward you, to protect you from them—

than it was for me to turn and face you.

Safer.

∽

For a brief period when I was fifteen, you and I sat with coffee and tea in the living room on Saturday mornings to talk for hours in our pajamas.

It was the small window, in the time of day and a period of life of my getting a need met from you.

You are a morning person, and so am I—and both of us love to talk.

"Let's have a visit," you would say. And shuffling with tea and coffee in hand, we would make our way into the living room.

"So, how are you?" you would ask—and that open, chatty tone in your voice would invite me into a conversation I so wanted to have.

Those morning conversations were reminiscent of the way I'd been able—*or was it that you'd asked me?*—to stay up late when I was a little girl, about five or six, to drink decaf coffee while you waited for Dad to come home from the hospital.

I don't think you liked to be alone.

Saturdays would pass by as the morning made its way into the day, and the sun would stretch slightly longer shades onto the floor and across the furniture, warming the room into the early afternoon, as we remained planted in those same weekly seated spots, softening the couch cushions through our wearing, as the hours of conversation went by.

I let myself open up to the feeling good with you, *just for a moment and however temporary*—in those places where only a conversation between mother and daughter can lead.

To have your attention and interest in what I was doing, or what I was thinking about someone or something, in the brightness of your morning moods—felt like being fed to me.

Eventually, the attention would fade, and the conversation always had a way of returning to you.

It is the same, today.

As I grew more into my adolescence, the competitiveness I could sense without language when I was younger also grew clearer.

Like the oil-thick brushes you held in your hand while you sat painting in your studio, I too became a canvas for you to paint your own parts upon, as you coated layers upon layers of mixed colors with long, hard strokes you then edged out with the sharpness of a palette knife.

"You're not an artist. I'm the artist."

"I'm the creative one."

"I'm the athlete."

"I, I, I . . ."

Your harsh looks grew into cruel-spirited sputterings of the things you said I was or wasn't.

One day, you praised me for being just like Dad—"You're so responsible, Christina"—and the next, degraded me for my dadlike plans for the future—

"You shouldn't go into medicine like your father. You'd have to actually work with people. Maybe you should work in a morgue instead."

One day up—"You're so naturally gorgeous!"

One day down—"You look sickly! Put on some makeup or something!"

Smart, hardworking—"I'm so proud of you, Christina, you're my golden child."

To terrible, disgusting, and annoying—"You're so ridiculous and self-righteous. Suck a joke . . ."

Physical degrading—"Look at your legs. Oh my God . . ."

To disgust on your face, after another night of fighting with "soulmate"—"You think you're Little Miss Perfect."

And silence, staring out the window, ruminating—"Screw you, Christina," under your breath . . .

I don't think there was ever a right way for me to be.

And there was no safe way for me to be with you, either.

Mostly, I kept myself hidden from you. Not wanting to risk what that openness could bring.

I know that when all else boils down, no one ever sees anyone as they truly are. That *"through a glass we* [all] *see darkly."*

But most people can see clearly enough.

You maneuvered people from within a room.

Brilliantly, beneath the radar.

Like a harsh cruelty within itself.

When my friends came over to the house, you would pretend to be another one of the teenagers as you greeted and fawned over them with compliments. Acting like I wasn't even in the room.

You told them they were *so tall and thin—*
　　　had *such beautiful, thick brown hair—*
　　　and were *so tough, and athletic.*

"Just like me," you'd say with a sigh.

Your compliments had a way of looping passively back to a way you had put me down before, where the subtlety and indirect route of wounding couldn't be seen by others. I became visibly hurt and would call you out when you joined me on the side of the room and listen, as you feigned your innocence.

"Ugh! I was not being mean!"

"This doesn't have anything to do with you, my God!"

"What's your problem?!"

What is wrong with you, Christina?

Eventually, moving back into the mix of people, you would look at my face, sadly subdued and flat from across the room, and laugh lowly.

"Let's get her," you said, looking at me, trying to sound playful. But I braced.

Standing beside one of my friends, gaining passive strength in numbers, you leaned against the counter, with a smile on your face, a glass of wine in hand.

Then you scoffed slightly, as red began to fill my growing shame, and tears pressed to well up in my eyes. "Oh, God, Christina, come on. Don't get upset," you smiled.

With my friends standing by, uncomfortably—now everyone silent, and holding their breath—the room was full of discomfort, and quiet.

I didn't know what to do.

Eventually, the Saturday mornings stopped.

I began to spend more nights with my trainer at the barn, and in the homes of my two best friends.

It was the beginning of my distancing
        and getting away.

Certain meaningful paradigms have taken on more cultural prominence in the last decade.

Trauma. Harm. Abuse.

Maybe we're more willing now to name what those in your generation never would.

I remember the afternoon that I went flying through the air, and into the corner edge of the couch.

When you shoved me, out of nowhere.

Moments before, I had been in the sitting room in the front of the house with Grandma, who had come to live with us after having a stroke.

I was sixteen and happy that afternoon, simple and content, as I told her about my day at school and the drama play I was auditioning for later that week. Sitting on her bedside in that calm, dipped place of late afternoon, a spring day of outside quiet all around. I heard you call my name from the other room.

I didn't even know you'd come home.

"Christina, come here." I heard a slight edge in your voice.

I touched Grandma's leg, and told her I'd be right back as I stood to walk to the living room to see why you were calling me.

"Yeah?" I asked, as I came toward you.

There was barely a moment between entering that room, my feet stepping onto the dark softness of the carpet, and when it happened—from out of nowhere, in an absence of any great warning. I can still feel the tenderness on my chest, where you gave me a few warm-up shoves—"bitch," "little shit," "self-right-eous," "what the fuck is your problem"—

before you really went for it and shoved me across the room.

It felt contaminating, to be leaning against the dirtiness of that couch, always smelling damp and constantly covered in dog hair.

Shaking uncontrollably. Terrified.

And how I was unable to really comprehend—then, and maybe even now—what had brought on the rage.

I'd barely seen you for days, because I was going to school, and you were off somewhere with our stepdad . . .

I tried to find a way to catch my brain up to what had happened that afternoon, but I never really made it.

You and he, drunk in the afternoon.

You usually were. Proof of your crutches were always laying around in the empty beer bottles that sourly profused themselves from beneath the couch. Coffee cups filled with wine. Cigarette ash along the glass coffee table, once a new and upscale piece of furnishing.

The two of you must have been on good terms together that day and needing someone else to take the blame for the incoherent rage you tossed between you like hot explosive sandbags that otherwise leaked at the seams.

But then part of me was beginning to understand enough to know: there didn't need to be sense or sanity to what was happening.

All it would take was some idea spun out of control, some misfired belief or gesture that could provide relief. To find someone else at fault for something of the dark mind. Whatever had gone on in the moments that led to that eruption, the emotional turmoil that flew around uncontained; it wouldn't matter what I did—

you would find your own justification.

Bam.

The hatred upon your face.

Sweating, beads of a dripping craze melting down your temples, eyes blaring, so much rage.

Breath close to my face, stench of ether and stale Marlboro—
a wiring insanity was coming off you, *at me.*

"Soulmate" stood in the corner, leaning against the wall, with his arms crossed. Drunk and content.

You looked me straight in the eye as I barely held myself upright from slipping on the edge of that couch from where you had
shoved me, trying not to fall.

And then you said it.

"I hate you, Christina."

I couldn't even breathe.

And then, it was over.

You both left and walked out of the room, proud of your-
selves.

"Stupid little bitch," echoed through the house as you walked
down the hallway.

Grandma called in the next room, unable to walk, saying,
"Christina? What's wrong?"

I flew out the front door, the screeching screen slamming behind
me—

   my head and my body moving at warping speeds, just not
    in the same line together.

Speeding across the grass of my best friend's front lawn. I was
allowed to come in through the garage door without knocking,
and so I did—and flew to her bedroom upstairs. Only needing to
get to somewhere safe,

   covered,

    and unseen . . .

And once I did, collapsed on her bedroom floor.

Shaking. Tears and snot everywhere, and me not understanding.

The pastel pink of that soft, tufted carpet. Gasping for air, and
sobbing through my head pains at the helplessness and insanity
of it all.

Sobbing at not being able to predict that this was coming, and of not being able to escape it all the same.

That day was the only time in my life that I ever gestured violently toward myself.

Finger pointed toward my temple, thumb raised, trigger and a click—

"*Bang!*" I cried.

Nothing I could do.

And, of course, the devastation that followed, when I confronted that *maybe I should just die*—

as my best friend sat cross-legged on the floor, my head in her lap, her hand upon my head, both of us crying—and she said,

"If you talk this way,

I'm going to need to get somebody else to help."

❩

I moved out when I was eighteen years old, and found an apartment in the city, where I lived alone.

A few years later, at twenty-one, I stopped having contact with you for a while.

I know I was exhausted from the ongoing ruptures, the malnourished or altogether absent repairs, and the growing sense that I no longer wanted to tolerate living with the cost being close to you took. Even in all my distance . . .

I know my needing to leave hurt you, and I'm sorry that it did—

but I'm not sorry that I left.

Leaving you in that larger way was what saved me, and saves me still. Even when I come back to these memories over the years, and try again to repair in my mind what's been severed as I feel the pull of your attempt to guilt me that cannot outweigh my determination to live, but which stems from the false notion that to love is to be loyal to the lie: that one must take care of the other who has harmed them.

And I think to myself, in the center of my spirit:

I had to go—

I had to find a better way to be who I really am.

I had to leave, wanted to leave, needed to leave—in order to survive.

Do you understand, Mom?

Do you know that I didn't *want* to, but *had* to?

That I needed to run, in order to take care of myself?

We're supposed to take care of ourselves, to pull all the broken pieces together to make something meaningful of the mosaic and get through life.

Right?

Mom???

I didn't tell you that I got cancer when I was twenty-five, even though we'd slowly begun having minimal and intermittent contact. Because I needed to stand silently and unperturbed in the shock of receiving the same diagnosis that Dad had died from.

For a moment, I considered reaching out—but the anger and fear I was confronting in that debilitating shock of a malignancy was not something I was willing to push aside in order to attend to you.

In the part of me that so longed to be comforted, I remembered: how quickly my need to be held while I sobbed would become about soothing *your* needs, *your* anxieties, and *your* worries.

I couldn't handle that.

And so, I waited until the cancer had been cut out and everything was clear, before diminishing the relevance of its ominous arrival, and telling you about it in a way that wouldn't tip you over, or cause a familiar spiraling of anxiety.

❧

As I looked at a framed picture of gold-colored, dried leaves you had given me when I turned sixteen hanging on the wall above my mahogany desk, I was warm within myself and my home, and quietly content.

It was fall, our family's beloved time of year, and the brown leaves were scurrying around the wet concrete of rain-slicked city streets. I lived in an old turn-of-the-century brick building just down the street from a small French bakery, and inside, sitting nestled on my couch, the lamps dimmed low, an old vintage run beneath my feet and a blanket strewn across my lap, I watched the evening light dip darker in the blue amid the glow of the gentle streetlights outside.

Despite the barriers, our love for some rarely fades. It was a year-and-a-half after my diagnosis, and with my heard relaxed, and open, I'd found that my mind began making its way toward you. I stood and walked across the cedar floors in bare feet to sit at my desk.

Words flowed with ease from a comforted place inside as I told you how much I loved you, and how I so appreciated your having passed on a way of arranging a home which I carried with me into the harmony of my own surroundings.

I told you that your giftedness for making a house a home was something I had always cherished.

"It always makes me feel good—carrying this part of you with me," I wrote.

And with a serene glow, I sent the letter away to you in the night.

You never responded.

I sat on the edge of my bed one night not long after, the low hue of a back ally streetlamp lighting parts of my bedroom in the dark as the rain poured down thick and rhythmic outside the open window. A few accumulated drops pattered together slowly on the ledge, and I called to see if you had received my letter.

I think I thought that you would have been happy to have received an offering of love—

and that you would have embraced my small attempt to respond, following years of you asking me to come back, when you had reached to me but I wouldn't let you in.

But when you picked up the phone, your voice was flat and withholding on the line.

After a pause, you said, "What, Christina?"

I could hear the tone of flat anger deep from the inside of my bones.

"I just wanted to see if you got the letter I sent you . . ."

I think I still assumed that honest moments of loving could somehow cross the gaps of disconnection and dispersion if what was offered was real and true. That loving could amend and transcend what had been broken apart, like a healing balm to bring back together what had once felt lost due to some ineffectual glue.

You remained quiet on the other end of the line and I could hear you breathing. And then, what was broken just broke further . . .

You went from silent withholding to telling me that you'd recently almost hurt yourself—because of the harm I had caused in my need to step away. A recent underplayed story from Toey about you taking some pills with too much wine and passing out while the stove was still on, and him coming home to a kitchen of smoke resurfaced in my memory . . .

I paused, and then you screamed, "DO YOU KNOW WHAT YOU ALMOST MADE ME DO!"

My heart—once subtly open—condensed sharply inward, closing, my stomach jerking into a queasily twisted knot, while my hand gripped the phone, and I once again became still and silent with shallow breathing.

I recognized the familiar inability for the conversation to go any further.

And, nausea quietly arising within me, my hands began shaking uncontrollably and I hung up the phone.

ʗ

You've written me your own letters over the years. Some have been filled with rageful accusation and violent hate, while others have offered apologetic utterances, attempting to mend the break.

And a few more still have offered some words of love.

The sadness is whatever sorriness you offered from within was a comfort, and validation—but the remorse itself never took root long enough to create lasting change.

I know the moments when you've loved me with certain pureness. I've felt them to be real, and tangible, and true. I still hold these memories in the place of my palm today, for the small illustrations of mothering they really are.

Perhaps all that matters is the semblances of love I have known from you, even if so much less than I wanted, infused our greater connection together—and not whether love can cross the divide "to make the wounded whole."

Moments of love can be so fleeting . . .

Even so, I'm not sure the unpredictability is worthy of making the experiences themselves any less real . . .

I will not cut off the love *you have offered*, even though I have often had to walk away . . .

In the years of my life with you, it has been the collapses following tender moments of love, that have often left me hungry, while bracing against residual memories of fear for a substance only you can give.

I eventually found deep riches within my ability to nurture myself, to decipher between what is strong rather than harsh, and what is sensitive and tender but not unreliable or weak.

But we only have one mother, whose literal cord feeds what will eventually nurture the figurative petals which flower when we accept all that we must learn to grow for ourselves. I found that seed with my own spirit, and found a way to feed myself.

And I may never be able to outgrow the trembling the harm your love left within me.

It is true that today—we don't know each other very well.

Maybe we never did.

Once in a while, I stop by, when I feel equipped enough to handle whatever comes my way. Sometimes connection finds a way to form between us, and for just a moment, some laughter erupts deep from within me, in a way that can only come from a certain exchange with you. Over lunch at an old restaurant, or when I'm seated with my hand resting upon our old kitchen table; I again feel the semblance of the home I came from that I sometimes miss and even long to return to without fully knowing why.

When the conversation goes well, there is a settling comfort that arises from a place only belonging to family that no one else can fill—and it warms me, and helps me to *re-member* pieces of what we once were. It is not only the bad that holds us together, even though we are mainly broken apart.

Soon, the moment is gone.

I am left to confront what remains unfinished.

My own forgiveness toward you, however partial, staggering and incomplete, always leaves me wanting to heal a little further, a little faster, in order to move back toward you again . . .

I remind myself of my often-misplaced responsibilities to heal what has come before me. And I settle back into the norm I have found of some safe-enough distance, and trying, ever further, to forgive and to let go.

The distance settles me into a fuller expression of who I know I really am. And I can breathe there, without worry, or fear.

But I am always left with that that deep, unutterable ache, as I drive away from you . . .

The way I know we don't always get what we want.

All that is between us, places broken off—
    snapped, green branches, the incomplete bloom—
    amidst the loss that exists within myself—and the empty
    spaces between you and me—
        I am searching, and fighting,
            alone in a dark womb,
        for specks of what is genuine between us.

The granules are hard to find . . .

I try and let illusions go, setting down my reach. Attending instead to the under-earth beneath my feet, where I try to gather all of myself—

amid incongruent waters, where I long to glide but not
be pulled beneath—
to someday swim within a congruent whole.
Then, that day, I may be able to say to you again—so clear,
and honest, with *open* love:
How it is that *I love you.*

Tonight, you called me on my way home from the grocery store,
and I answered and pulled off the drive of an old dirt road. Elbow
hanging out an open window, I watched the ending of the day, as
it dropped further away—
and the rays dappled on the leaves, amid the golden green.
Branches swayed as the sense of summer's ending blew gently
in the wind, and my small, bare feet were perched atop the dash-
board as you spoke—
when distant memories, echoes of your voice in the past,
rang mocking jokes of laughter.
Hurt for a moment, I felt a quick and sudden need to hide—
when I then breathed deep the country air, so clean and
sweet and warm—as your voice chattered away on
the end of the line.
Sensations of wild and quiet life flowed in and around me, and
I knew that fall was coming. Soon, more memories began to
dance, and I was carried home after school in junior high, where
you stood in the kitchen cooking dinner atop the old antique
stove as the sound of classical music played in the background,
and a feeling of warmth and happiness took hold of me from
within time in space. The sun that shone now through the dap-
pling of leaves upon my legs was the same light that brightened
the childhood home of my past that fall, many years ago. It
sprawled throughout the inside walls of our country-yellow home,

warming the floors, covering the wood cabinets, as its rays poured sharply through a steady glass of wine sitting still upon the marble countertop as you stirred and smelled your spaghetti sauce simmering for dinner. You greeted me joyously, "Hi, Anna," while Toey was upstairs, and Dad was driving alone on his way back home from work . . .

I closed my eyes and remembered that speck of memory— that small moment in time when everything felt alright *enough*. I watched the reel go by, as I tore a piece of French bread from the brown baker's bag, dipped it within the sauce, and ate.

I opened my eyes.

The conversation that day then grew reminiscent—our old Saturday mornings, and we laughed, turning to stories of the past, and I felt us align and then diverge to separate landings, while a cool line of wind suddenly chilled my skin as it changed from the once warm breeze.

Where there are differences between us, so many, in the ways we see each other and view the past—

I've become better now: at breathing and noticing.

I do not need to disjoint when I am in your presence—the way that I once had.

In the places you are unable to acknowledge what has happened, how what was done ripples within me throughout the years—and the places where you are unable to see or acknowledge me at all.

I am *okay enough* in the aloneness of that now,
> when I am with you,
>> and the open, raw grief that comes from an unsewn
>>> wound whenever we are unable to touch
>>>> and know each other
>>>>> as we really are.

You laughed on the other end of the line at something which now I can't remember, and I was looking at the leaves on the trees out the window, with tears in my eyes.

Mustard Seeds

— Jaxon —

There can be subtle humor in the ordinary.

The way you can cross paths with someone who will become a significant chapter in your life—and despite the relevance and meaning between you, all the healing and transformation you will have in your time together—

you can still manage to meet them, waiting in a line,

just to get a burger.

All I wanted was a gluten-free salmon burger.

And a Coke. On ice.

I was standing cross-armed in a line that should have been short, if altogether nonexistent—but instead spanned almost out the door. It was the bus of students; I think they were from out of town. I was irritated. It was the time of night that usually brought quiet to this part of town—eight o'clock, Thursday, in a completely undeveloped neighborhood, in the bone-cold middle of February.

I banked on the quietness.

And the expectation was failing me.

I was one month away from leaving a job that, despite my hopes, had *not* turned out to be the one.

Research was not my calling in the world.

And my relationship with the painter had eye-openingly ended, four months before, when I discovered what it meant to hit my rock-bottom.

Tired, seeping pain, discouraged, and pissed off, I was harboring humbly on my psychic bottom floor. And yes—

while those are the places where deep healing typically begins—

and while life *usually* finds a way to bring us to the healing we need—

all I wanted that night was my salmon burger.

Obviously, I knew there were people in front of me, they were the reason for my elongated wait and annoyance. But the individuality of everyone was obscured by my fatigue. So, I didn't even notice that there was "someone"—*in front of me*—in the line.

But there you were, now turning around, out of nowhere, and talking to me.

I inwardly rolled my eyes. *What the fuck does this guy want?*

Keeping my arms crossed, I glanced at you from the side of my eye, so as not to be *overly* rude—but also to remain flat and ineffectual.

Don't flirt with me. I'm not in a good mood.

You kept talking! And so, fine, I couldn't dismiss the sky-pierced blue of your eyes, the well-parted haircut, your arm, covered entirely in black tattoos, stemming all the way to an inked symbol stitched onto your middle finger . . .

Alright, there might be something interesting here. But . . .

Too JCrew . . .

And you work at a large corporation?

(Ew).

Yeah, yeah, that's nice—(!) You were just promoted.

Leave me alone.

If I'm being honest, the truth is that the energy it takes to dislike someone is fairly exhausting. So yes, I eventually softened. And stopped bracing against your unanticipated presence.

By the time we had our bags, paper crumbling under our grip, and napkins in hand (*forty-five minutes later*), a number was exchanged—"Cider, sometime?"—I inclined, we departed and went our separate ways. I drove in the black, mine and the night's, toward the nurturing and dim-lit office of a woman with a medicinal presence who offered just the right balance of blunt honesty and gentle holding to see me through the "healing crisis" I was in. When my spirit would unravel all its honesties at the end of those weeks when I went to meet her . . .

As I attempted, with nowhere farther to run, to make meaning of my life's themes and scenes.

When I think of the way it felt venturing out to see you that first time, I can still feel the calming in my cells.

The way that even before seeing you, I had this hinting sense of your *reliability*.

Driving down the street to another part of town, deep, dark, and cold outside, but blazing warm in my overheated vehicle (just the way I preferred), I had a flash—that you would be at the restaurant, already there to meet me.

Even though we'd hardly spoken since that first night; something in me knew that you would be waiting.

Drawing from the cold into dim lighting and a gentle oriental melody, the aroma of broth and herbs warmed my insides. I saw you stand from a table in the back, blonde hair, a darkened, solid figure of subtle intensity, black sweater and jeans, so attractive and contained, holding it all inside.

I'd never been to a pho restaurant before. Vegetables simmered in their deepened mahogany broth and basil leaves floated green alongside the side of my smooth wood chopsticks. The nervousness that exists between two early strangers held its own electrical charge, but around that subtle *zimmering*, I felt simultaneously calmed from the inside out.

You paid the bill and we walked down the street to sip ciders as promised in a nearby earth-toned bar. The fermented ether greeted my throat and swept down into my heart space. I tasted yours—musky, not my preference; and you, mine—sweet, which wasn't yours. We sat with our different tastes, alongside each other, arms resting on the long, stretching, mahogany wood of the warm-lit counter.

I found out through the evening that you were my age. You told me about growing up in Arizona, joining the Army just out of high school, and about your punk rock days. Dabbling in anarchist ideology for a time. You didn't go to college. Two previous relationships. And one younger brother, with whom you had a particularly difficult connection. You worked in an organic grocery store before moving on to becoming an escalation specialist in the global security control center of a corporate office.

There were no drugs, no heavy drinking—such a reprieve from the alcoholism of my previous lover that mimicked the roots of my family origins.

It was clear that you took care of your responsibilities, and I could see, as well, your body.

You were smart.

And I felt resonance toward your evasion of more traditional routes in life—whether they were academic, ideological, or relational.

You were also a concentrated and good listener.

Walking beside me with a slight stiffness in your hip, after sitting on those hardened bar chairs, you hugged me goodnight in the cold.

You told me you'd call me next week—

    but you never did.

I'd just moved into a small brick building in a new part of town, a quaint corner apartment that filled with morning light, where an oak tree stood rooting itself through grass outside the front window.

I sat my small patio table and chair under the branches of that tree. And through the tall, wide windows of that small, open space, every morning flew the singing sound of birds.

A small bakery was only a short walk away, and just behind the bend, a cemetery sat silent—filled with enormous overarching maple trees, standing wisely over quietly laid graves of grass and walkways sacred, not meant to be trampled.

The streets I walked along were quiet and peaceful, as I brushed my fingers along the leaves and flowers of gardens blooming, gently tapping my hands atop the white-post fences.

I'd recently been accepted to get my master's degree in psychology and decided to leave my ill-fitting job in research for a few months of reflection and rest before the coming academic absorption and rigor. I continued with my own personal healing, grueling and freeing as it was in its processes of acknowledgments and surrenders. Doing so required me to discover new kinds of rest and develop previously unknown rhythms after sessions where I'd released old and turbulent waters within myself. I accompanied various body and craniosacral work with the emotional and psychological, while I taught early morning cycling classes at a gym and read books on *the desert fathers* and *vocational calling* while sitting in my small, yellow paisley chair in the corner by the window, where I could feel the gentle touch of the breeze.

It was the paradigmatic shift in my life away from paths that would not feed to the self-sustaining work within that enriches. The early days of large, gut-wrenching, honest work of psychospiritual resifting that asks us to slowly remove the circumstances that distract us from tending to the original wounds within.

And to land in our lives, wherever we really are.

I thought of that place as my healing apartment . . .

And when all that I was doing was good but still not good enough, that cemetery was only a short walk away.

There, I snuck through the bushes and onto the wandering grass, delicately searching and finding my place to lie, descending atop the earth. Secluded and alone. The grassy softness holding and accepting that which other hands and voices of wisdom had been unable to get to in that time of honest and beautiful cracking open.

I waited for you to call, knowing you'd gone out of town on a road trip with some guys. When you didn't, I sent you a message—

"Hey J, was just thinking of you. How was your trip?"

We met later that week, on the busyness of an afternoon street in the same part of town as our interminable burger line.

That day we kissed for the first time.

For a moment I lingered, and then noted when you nervously pulled back, as if somehow aware of the public exposure in our surroundings. I couldn't care less about the bustle, but was intrigued all the same . . .

And later, found out why.

The following Sunday, I had you over for dinner at my apartment where I stood cutting vegetables in my tiny and recently repainted rectangular kitchen.

I was happy that day: light and fresh and airy. The beginning of spring was only days away, and daylight was beginning to spread farther into the early hours of the evening. My birthday was nearing, and I felt myself coming alive.

My eyes were watering from the onions I was chopping on top of the narrow kitchen counter. Never having been hesitant to get to the point of what I want to know, I asked whether you were seeing anyone else. As you drew in a short breath, I remained casually focused on the vegetables, calmly stirring sliced red and green bell peppers through warming olive oil.

I kept mostly quiet, as I took in that you were seeing someone—it was "casual" and you both "saw other people"—though it was still your "primary relationship." I turned down the burner and added the remaining thin slices of garlic from the counter, everything sizzling gently, releasing a caramel-sweet aroma as I rinsed sleek-watered remnants from my hands.

When I broke things off with you a few days later, I did so as a gift to myself. On the day before my twenty-eighth birthday. I knew then that moving toward someone who wasn't available would only lead me to rehash old patterns, which felt like reaching for scraps, rather than something that could actually nourish.

I sat in my car at one of my favorite beach places across from town by the edge of the water as I found the simple words to say that I really liked you, but the circumstances weren't a good fit for me. I told you that if things changed, to let me know.

Your response came much slower than usual.

But you said that you understood.

The months went by, spring stretching into early summer.

I continued diving into my own waters, coupling inner work with the theoretical perspectives I was learning in graduate school as I read books on beauty and tragedy, Celtic mysticism, and the gifts of different therapeutic approaches.

You remained in my thoughts, hovering and floating around. We sent a few messages from time to time—"read this book and thought of you"—met, exchanged a book, and then went our separate ways.

By midsummer, you were no longer involved with anyone, and we went kayaking one afternoon in July.

I felt then that if I was honest with myself and safe, I was free to let things be simply as they were.

Feeling free and safe came easily with you.

So, as we sat on the outdoor patio of a restaurant on the lake, our kayaks tied on the dock nearby, as the sun sprinkled bright orange-yellow flares of light off the afternoon water, with chopsticks in my hand and a piece of salmon dipping into ginger soy sauce, I said directly and casually before taking the bite—

"So, do you think we should have sex?"

You nearly choked on your sushi.

Nettle tea with raw honey, and oatmeal topped with chia seeds and cranberries for breakfast followed nights slept close by your side. We would walk arm-in-arm down the street from your apartment to a nearby coffee house, where I would read Mary Oliver, journal, and sip English Breakfast with cream, while you glanced quietly over the newspaper with a black Americano in what I was quickly recognizing to be your very constricted (*ahem, grumpy*) morning mood.

But you were a relief from the turbulent years before.

Even when you were held far in, reluctant to accept simple reflections of how I felt, seated atop your bathroom counter, when I told you that—*you were a solid and good man*—while you brushed your teeth late one evening.

"I feel so vulnerable and exposed," you said, laughing, mouth covered in toothpaste.

I smiled, knowing vulnerability doesn't negate solidity.

We spent that summer together as the green began turning amber in the passing toward fall, the two of us becoming more and more familiar.

With the growing familiarity, you began to relax your serious side . . .

One afternoon, as I sat at your small kitchen table in the stretching rays of sun, I looked up as your voice lowered into a growl while you spread ingredients over a sandwich.

"*Mustard . . .*" you said hoarsely.

The orange-brown condiment scooped from the jar as the knife clicked the inside the brim.

My eyes widened with surprise. Then I glanced to the black-and-white Clint Eastwood poster on your wall.

An impersonation?

Okay . . .

"You're a Mustard." I said back.

"*Spicy. Stone ground.*" Gruffly, twisting the lid of the jar closed.

Oh my god, he's being goofy . . .

I looked up and sighed. "Well fine. Then I'm *Honey Mustard.*"

Tilting my nose slightly up in the air, and closing my eyes with aristocratic contentment while you quietly repeated "Honey Mustard," as your head dipped behind the refrigerator door.

Thus began the inside jokes of endearment nobody ever finds funny but for the two people involved.

In October, when the crimson leaves blew as they dangled from rain-splattered branches, and the cold of the air settled in a hovering fog amid the foliage, you told me, your eyelids bequeathing tears, that you had decided to take a job in Arizona, where you were from.

It appeared that you needed to discern, though it was not without ambivalence, whether the landscape of the hardened desert floor with its floating tumbleweeds and dust-filled air was where you belonged.

I asked you to stay.

You cried, unsure of yourself. And, then, left anyway.

"Friends back home. Money, stability, potential for growth . . ." Sometimes, we have to go back in order to go forward. To find where it is we don't want to be, in order to discover where we do.

I cried the afternoon you left, alone on the deep green grass of those comforting graves and spiritually overhanging leaves in the wind.

❧

From the cool, dark green evergreens of the Northwest to the prickling cacti and pine trees of the desert, our relationship grew in a deeper way through distance. We flew overarching miles every other month to see each other, and ended each of the days in-between, our voices on the other end of the telephone.

When winter came, you went missing in the Superstition Mountains one Sunday afternoon.

"I'll call you about one-thirty this afternoon, your time," you said, just before setting out to hike after yoga with some friends.

But one-thirty that afternoon quickly came and went.

By eleven-thirty that night, the minutes scathing by, stretching, building scurrilously on top of one another, your absence evoked flashing images from violent meetings on the path, to lostness, broken bones, unconsciousness in dirt-filled ditches, and venomous reptilian desert blood running through your sweating veins.

I can be resourceful when necessary. Not knowing any of your friends' last names, and knowing that you weren't on any online social platform that could help link me to available help, I reverse-traced my way to one of your oldest friend's wives via the name of a business venture she undertook in the area. It took me thirty-five minutes to link the names together and conclude it was her. After I found her social media account and sent her a message, she called me fifteen minutes later. Her sister was hiking on the path with you, and we were both growing more concerned.

I was hitting the numbers to dial Search and Rescue when my phone rang—

"We took a wrong turn . . ." It was your voice, breaking up from poor reception, standing on a nearby highway, where you were calling from a gas station with a dwindling single bar of battery left on your phone.

My fiery reactivity quickly settled in relaxation and relief— even though you took me right up to the edge of my panic when I thought you disappeared.

Even though you were alright, all along.

Spring came, and we traveled to acres of red-and-yellow tulip fields spread far and wide. The mud covered my green boots and squished as I stepped through rows of flowers, my cold fingers rolled into a ball inside your warm hand wrapped around mine. We walked through antique stores and sat sipping cider and beer at country restaurants, and, sensing your growing discontent with the Arizona desert, I asked the same question I had been thinking in the months since you'd left—

"So, when are you coming back?"

At the end of June, nearly one year after our kayaking excursion, all of my first-year papers and exams completed, I flew, relieved and exhausted, down to the scorching sun of the desert, where heatwaves rising off pavement burned the pads of my feet and my eyes watered—and we filled a yellow Penske truck with your belongings. You moved back to the Northwest and into an apartment I'd tracked down for you and one of your oldest guy friends along the small streets of the same beach town where I had earlier ended our involvement.

A month later, I moved in with you, too. That new space replaced the quiet of my healing apartment's breeze-whispered mornings with the occasional sound of cars driving by and a few plumbers from the business next door yelling out profanities to one another from the other side of the fence.

I found new birds who sung from the curving branches of the oak tree in our small backyard or along the wirelines that crossed through the air of the back alley, and other warming influences came to fill what had been left behind by that small apartment by the cemetery trees.

From the bottom of the stairs in the morning, I called upward—

"Muuuuuuustard . . ."

Silence.

"I made you coffee!"

I'm awake. Wake up!

My hand rested on the railing of the stairs, and I quieted my breathing so as not to miss your stirring in bed . . .

A single groan from the room. "Okay."

Pause.

"I'll be there in a minute."

Always fussy in the morning. You'd begun to add a little more emphasis to your "grumpy" voice ever since I'd pointed it out the summer prior, and I gave you a blend of both compensatory attention and space . . .

Loving the early bright of day, I smiled and skipped over to the counter before sliding in my socks toward the breakfast I had laid out on the counter for us both: two bowls with oatmeal, chia seeds, and cranberries beside a mug of coffee and cup of tea. I left your coffee aero-pressed and dripping in the large, oversized graduate school memorabilia mug you had bought me in my first year of school, which you now used more than I did.

I picked up my bowl, warm on the edges, put it on top of my teacup, and opened the backdoor to the patio balcony, where I set everything down on the small table that had once sat beneath the tree outside my other apartment. Living on a tight budget, I painted cinderblocks lime green and laid single slats of wood to make benches for flower boxes, which now began to bloom into color, and softly blew their bright, pink-and-yellow petals in the saltwater breeze. A wooden lattice stood tall by the railing, helping to block the view of the plumbers' trucks on the other side of the fence.

I kept the backdoor open and followed the sunlight pouring into the kitchen as I went back inside to grab a poetry book, and, placing it beneath my arms, with my journal in hand, left the door open as I sat cozily into one of the chairs looking over the morning—and you descended the stairs, while I began sipping my tea, clanking my spoon against my oatmeal bowl, and singing a melody of gladness into the new day.

Being at home with you was a time of real joy.

The months passed throughout the year and the days grew dark and cold in winter. And I began to sense, from our moving more deeply together, that I felt afraid.

They were the fears, I recognized, of *early experiences* of life.

I had never lived with anyone, having moved out when I was only eighteen, and had for eleven years lived on my own. Now, twenty-nine years old, I was nestled into a space with two boys in an old, two-bedroom apartment. Living in a different side of the city from what I was used to. Away from my comforts of my quiet streets and grassy grave lands.

I was grateful for the theoretical compass of my graduate studies, coupled with therapeutic work, which gave me some idea of what was emerging while I felt ajar and my mind wondered what was going on as I began to feel *panic in closeness, desires for safety,* and *terror of depending on another person.* Feelings of old dread arose from within my cells and spread into the present.

Should I be here?

Is he going to hurt me?

Should I leave?

Who is this person?

I should go. It isn't safe.

Am I safe?

Sitting in the deep corner of our dark turquoise couch, alone in the apartment, I would hold myself beneath a blanket, knees pressed into my chest as those old origins would emerge, and I saw a string of moments weave themselves together through time.

I was struck that the only time the feelings emerged was in the late afternoon—around four o'clock. Then I remembered: that late time of afternoon was when I would wander home from school and be alone in the house as my dad lay dying of cancer on the couch.

And in my adolescent years that followed his death, it was also when my mom began to drink, and her moods begin to shift.

I then accessed life from an even earlier stage, where remnants of the depression my mom fell deep into after my brother was born emerged, when I was only three or four years old. A feeling of being remarkably alone in a house as a young child while she was somewhere downstairs flooded my body and I panicked, not trusting if anyone would come to get me.

Sensations as ghosts of another time, tracing themselves together in unanchored moments. I could feel their qualities—of infancy, adolescence, being a young child, early adulthood. Different memories moving timelessly through me from varying aspects of my life.

The *stretching hours of quiet aloneness in so many of our different homes growing up*—

   the *in-between time of the day after coming home from junior high school*—

   a wondering feeling—is Dad going to die today?

Sucking my thumb in a crib. Eyes staring up at a ceiling. *No one is around.*

Something feeling off and sad in the house as I stand at eleven years old on the stairs.

Terrorizing panic at sixteen at night, *I'm frozen beneath covers—but people are home?* Wondering, *why it is I think I am alone?*

And the sense I held in my body, of not even bothering to cry, because of some innate understanding—

that I may not be held, or found, if I did.

I heard a saying once, that "in the presence of real love, everything unlike love comes up for review."

The mysteries of our pasts arise in our closest encounters with others.

By the next spring we'd been living together for close to nine months, and I sat one Saturday afternoon in the sunny living room of a close friend's condo across town. I'd decided I needed to have a few days away, believing I needed to get some space *from you*, rather than the feelings that were arising within me in being *with* you.

I sipped tea on my friend's flowering couch and prayerfully contemplated. I was considering that perhaps I should skedaddle from the relationship; the anxiety I felt was that obviously we weren't a good match. We weren't always interested in the same things . . . We gravitated toward different social circles . . . I went to therapy—you barely did. (I took this as an *obvious sign* we were not compatible or in the same place . . . .)

Finding self-justification to avoid what we long to escape in ourselves is easy to come by if we circumvent our deeper realities.

I prayed for clarity, some *sign*, and as I did, felt completely resolute in my inner confidence that it was the *relationship* that was the problem, and that I should just go.

The acknowledgment relieved me, and I ventured lightly out into the morning to a dance class across town.

An hour-and-a-half later, when my kneecap jerkingly slid out from its socket and cracked open while floating dislocated on the outside of my leg under my skin, I wailed in pain at the awe of my body's shocking and unnatural disfiguration.

Laying on a hospital bed, a full-leg brace supporting my excruciating leg, after having had three residents hold me down while they straightened it back into place, I felt even through the anesthetics that there was something greater at work in my new-found inability to walk.

You came straight to the emergency room to find me and took me home.

And I lay on the couch, unable to even move without your help, for the following few weeks . . .

Unable to run away or release stress or anxiety through any of my normal outlets, I sobbed on the couch like a child filled with un-utterable frustration and longing for something I didn't know how to name.

You held me, concentrated, quiet, receptive, and still, and never tried to dislodge me from whatever I was sinking into.

The panic I had outrun for so many years settled into its origins—helpless, child-like worry over feeling close or dependent on you.

I was terrified that you would get angry at me for my basic needs, for not being able to move, or walk, or do anything I was independently able to before. You were working full-time, going to massage school, and taking care of everything at home. I had always been able to take care of myself and felt that if you grew upset over what I couldn't control, I would have no way to be able to leave in order to save myself—which was the option I always believed I needed.

You never even became a glimpse of my fears.

Placing my warm tea on the coffee table in the morning, you kissed me softly on the forehead before heading to work. And in the early evening, returned home to ask about my day as you made dinner and lit an orange spice candle we'd bought at one of our favorite breakfast spots in my hometown.

In those months of recuperating, I relaxed into you more fully. With your patient attentiveness and embrace, I released in that broken leg the hurts of so many other wounds of my life. Resting my head on your chest, unabated tears flowed from the earliest days of my life, never having been offered the holding they needed in order to let go. Eyes swollen with tears, snot running out of my nose, feelings from all my life poured through me. And all the while, a new experience deepened, as I learned the sensation of what real trust is—and that strength flushed old memories from my cells and replaced them with an innate understanding that to be really held is to be healed.

As I began restrengthening, struggling to get up and move again without the help of your steadying hand—you sat nearby with sturdy encouragement in the face of my frustration and impatience. Wobbling, as I learned, step-by-limping-step, to walk again.

Because of you, I found that I could fall, and find my way back up to move newly in life again.

We never return to "where we were" before an injury.

We only learn to move differently, knowing we have been changed.

A few weeks into my rehabilitation, I hopped one afternoon on my crutches to a bookshelf to read about the *meta* behind the *physical* of my injury. I flipped my way through a book on alternative interpretations of *knee problems* by Louise Haye. It read:

"Knee: Represents pride and ego. Stubborn ego and pride. Inability to bend. Fear. Inflexibility. Won't give in."

I rubbed my eyes and laughed at the not-so-subtle, loving humor of the divine.

⟡

Giving, in love, is not the same as receiving.

Throughout our relationship, there were times when I tried to tell you how I felt about you—as a man, and the importance of what you were to me.

But something came between us as you struggled to receive what I was offering.

"You're a good man . . ."

You would look down as I sat on your lap, facing you, and I saw in your eyes the way you withdrew to some deep, darkened place within yourself.

I knew then that there were places I wanted to reach in you that you did not want me to go. I could feel your boundary line, *too much* intimacy, and I softly kissed the sides of your eyes, rubbed my hand on your face, and rehabilitated enough to walk again, went to the kitchen to make you something for dinner instead.

I wanted to honor that unspoken guarding in you, sensing you were not ready to be more fully held yourself.

I replaced my spoken words with cursive shorthand instead and left them rolled and tied over rough recycled paper inside a sea-green glass bottle on the shelf I'd built by the door. Letters were the only way to give voice to my love amid your gentle need for silence—and to honor us both, in the oscillating need for closeness, and for space.

I left them waiting where you could reach for them, whenever you were ready.

ᥫ

A year passed.

We walked the beach strand alongside waves rolling in toward the shore one day, bright, sunny, and cold, a weekday morning in early winter. Commuters gone to work, there was nothing but a few morning walkers and seagulls passing overhead. I squeezed your arm, felt joyful and full of play. You were subdued, not wanting to participate in the smell of the breeze or smiling ponderings about life in the new day.

I sighed, and we walked arm-in-arm in our different felt places.

Your friend had moved out, and later that day when you opened the door after work, it was to an apartment in the midst of reassembly. You smiled endearingly and acknowledged what you knew your role was to be in the moving of things.

"Oh boy. How many times have I moved furniture in this house?"

I looked up at you, serious in my task, wide-eyed and playful all at once.

"*This* needs to be moved *there*," I said, pointing to whatever was too heavy for me to maneuver on my own.

And on we went, scooting, lifting, and sliding, with love in the heavy lifting. Your camouflage flip-flops chafing on the driveway as I stood on the balcony, serious-faced and eyebrow-furrowed, hands on my hips, deciding where to place a new planter pot.

Even in the smooth reconfiguring of that apartment, the truth is we began to notice differences between us that could perhaps not be moved.

Still, I left your favorite baked chips on the counter next to the sparkling water I'd bought for you at the store, and you would leave me dinner on the stove after I came home from a class on a heavier lecture night.

We adjusted to each other and slept in separate bedrooms from time to time, feeling it was important for us to have our own space.

In the morning, one of us would always crawl into bed beside the other: usually me. I would peak around the corner to where you lay covered in a quilted down comforter and stand at the door, smiling and biting my finger until you noticed I was there.

"Get in," you'd say, eyes still closed, and I'd excitedly crawl in beside you, warmed from your body heat under the covers, sliding the back of your heel between my first two toes, and squeezing into your back.

To acknowledge then, a few years in, that we may have transformed from lovers into something more familial and platonic seemed like a hard thing to bear. Our own families had never been solid places for either of us to land. Anyone who comes from vulnerable beginnings knows how that lack of security evokes an often vulnerable walk, not easily ignored.

The comfort, care, and stability we gave each other were our forms of loyalty and love.

I wondered if acknowledging the growing change between us and transforming the structure of our relationship could mean we would lose it all.

Safety and care are not always the only ingredients the heart longs for.

It was a habitual non-joke within an endearing joke, when I would say, "I'm never gonna forget about you."

The truth beneath that statement was that you had been missed or not seen by others too many times before . . .

To this day, the thought fills me with an ache, too out of reach for words.

Perhaps this is where the loss lies in you, as well—

far, but deep, and out of reach.

I know one of my greatest failures was the fact that I did, at times, *miss you too.*

That I didn't see you in all the ways you needed to be seen.

I know those moments hurt you.

They were my own failure, and my limitedness.

You would look at me with a constricted, stern look, filled with skeptical testing in your eyes from where you sat in a corner from across a room—and I would keep my gaze on you, not wavering, to convey the integrity behind my words.

I am right here.

And I still am.

ᏟᎾ

When I think of our relationship, I think of it as transforming into what it always was, and our discovering that landscape along the way.

I think of it also as the reality we face—when despite all of the meaning and healing we find with someone else, we are not always meant to go beyond what has already unfolded.

Each coming together has its own purpose: a way meant to work with the journeys our souls have signed up for.

Our purpose together is limited, perhaps, just as we are.

When we acknowledged the end of our romantic tie to each other, we decided to keep living together like the family we felt we were. We moved into separate bedrooms, updated our financial arrangements, and discerned the new social comings-and-goings respectfully toward each other.

I hung that contract up on the wall—our two signatures over a dotted line, wooden thumbtack pinned over country yellow paint, next to "Welcome Home" written on the chalkboard hung by the front door.

And then sat and drew leaves upon an old oak tree, each one a symbol for the new growth we had discovered between us.

"Trust."

"Safety."

"Reliability."

"Yams." (Yes, you told me I would love them . . .)

I pinned that drawing up on the wall as well—and we had those leaves to look to when we needed to see the good that had burgeoned between us.

When we needed to be reminded that what we had together was not a failure, even though a part of it was ending.

Today, it has been some years since we met in that quiet part of town.

After almost five years together, I moved to an apartment up the hill, and like the unfolding relationship between us, the move felt natural, timely, and gentle.

After another year of transition, I found my way farther to the home I have today.

Even with the tender undoing that came from spacing ourselves away from each other, it still took some time—

to clear the room you occupied in the comforting part of
my mind.

For a time, I trembled slightly as I questioned whether I could make it alone and learn to be alright without you. Leaning on each other gave us rest from the years that had tired our souls.

That leaning *strengthened us*, for a time.

After a while, if we don't learn again to stand erect, our resting muscles begin to weaken.

When we finally find the courage to stand,
    taller than before,
        we find we are changed.

It is not without a tender sadness,
    and relief,
        that we let go of that supporting hand . . .

What is love, if not something that *we follow*. It becomes whatever it is meant to be, and if allowed ushers us further inside the healing of ourselves.

We do not direct its course or direction.

Love is simply something we show up for.

You, for a time, my partner, and now, my friend, must know the deep rest and goodness that came from being with you, and how that serendipitous meeting *has healed my bones for the better.*

Thank you for giving me something to hold onto and take with me—so that despite whatever turbulences or loneliness may still exist in my life, I will always have the warmth and kindness of your love to remember.

Whatever distance is now meant to exist between us, know that I will always hold the truth of what I was able to know *within you—within me.*

You are a good man.
You are easy to love.

And I'm never gonna forget about you.
Mustard.

Sissy

— Christopher —

When you were little, you were this *giddy* little boy. And so obsessive!

I would walk into the living room and trip over your toy boats, lined in neat, precise rows on the carpet.

"Ouuww! Toey! Move your boats!"

My stumbling detoured the methodical journeys in between the islands of the Puget Sound, and you responded with deep frustration. "I lined them up, they're lined up, you messed them up! Sissy!" you whined back.

You could outline the entire San Juan Islands on those floors with a map inside your mind. As you pressed hard onto the floor, focusing, slowly moving each boat from one island to the next, leaving a wake of each vessel indented on the carpet. Throttling engine noises gurgling out from the little chamber in your throat, as you sailed steadily through pretend waters.

"Chuga-chuga-chuga-chuga . . ."

You stroked the tail of your graying, stuffed teddy bear in between your fingers, sucking your jaw up-and-down, as you lay on Mom's chest, cuddling. She smelled your hair and closed her eyes as she took you in.

I was six, and you were three. Already, Mom felt less soft to me; the way she patted my back a little too hard when I sat on her lap, rocking in the rocking chair—"ouch, Mom, that hurts . . ."—and how she pressed the bristles into the scalp of my head, brushing and tugging slightly as she combed through the strands of hair.

"Sorry," she'd say. But the uncomfortable brushing continued.

When I look back at you together, sitting on the couch and cuddling, I can see from an early age how you really needed her. And the way she felt differently toward you, perhaps, because of that need.

More nurturing.

You had a different relationship with Mom than I did—

and you still do.

I watched you be shy with others when we were young.

Sometimes, when approaching one of my own friends to play, I would ask them, "Can my brother come, too?"

I felt so protective of you, never wanting you to feel left out . . .

One thing Mom did so well was to nurture the strength of our bond as siblings. "I always wanted my kids to be close," she'd say.

And we were.

Making forts to hide between the couches with large, white sheets—and becoming best friends with the neighbors next door.

The four of us ran through the grass in our backyards, jumping into ditches, rolling to the ground, and hiding behind trees as we played in the hours after school . . .

Throughout the years of our childhoods, we slept side-by-side for comfort, when one of us became afraid. When fear or terror would approach in the dark, your soft voice would whisper at my door, "Can I sleep with you, Sissy?" Or, tiptoeing myself through the dark, shadowed halls of the night, peeking through your door. "Toey?" I'd whisper. "I'm scared."

Into the other's bed one of us would crawl. Even when you snored so loudly that you couldn't hear me, as I tucked beneath the sheets that were cold on the empty side—lying next to you always felt like a comfort when I was otherwise alone.

Even when I woke—as you struggled in bouts of fearful sleep, damp in sweat and encumbered in the terror of your dreams.

There's something uniquely satisfying about getting a younger sibling to do the things for you that you don't want to do for yourself. Maybe it's an inherent sibling dynamic to see how far you can push the bounds, or maybe it was just me being lazy, but when we were kids, I never wanted to get up for Kleenex whenever I was about to sneeze.

When I was ten years old, we lived in the country, surrounded by innumerable types of cumulating, combustive combinations of pollen that blew in the spring and summer air.

My allergies were the worst.

As I felt the eruption of histamine build within my chest, tingling up into my light-headed brain and down through my nose, I'd hit *pause* on the movie we were watching—

"Oh no. I'm going to sneeze . . ."

Arching back, thrusting forward, snot flying all over my face—

ACHHOO!

Really, what I liked to do was make the mess sound truly emergent—*deeply* serious—so I could get you to run for the Kleenex.

"Oh noo!" I sounded, despairing. "It's everywhere!"

I looked over at you with big, desperate eyes from where you sat on the chair beside me.

"Toey, can you get me a tissue???"

Anything but helpless, I still managed to get you to jump up from our swirling blue chair in front of the television, as I held my hands to my face to contain the ejected reactions to the pollen and grass, as you zoomed into the hallway toward the bathroom.

I could hear the jumbling of a small cardboard box followed by the swift pull of soft fabric that was followed by a little thump of feet on the hallway floor as you returned, running back from the bathroom.

"Here, Sissy!!!" you said, with your little voice so sweet and proud.

Wiping the mess: "Thanks, Toey," I said with a sigh.

You hopped back onto the chair beside me, and it bounced from our weight. We wiggled and adjusted, our shoulders and legs pressing against each other as our feet dangled and kicked slightly, and I twirled us around in circles, before pressing *play* and resuming our movie together.

During the short years of our youth, winter was enfolded by a magical veil of unseen, benevolent comfort.

Excitement glittered beneath glowing lights, as the weeks darkened further into the warmth of the enclosure that led us toward Christmas Day. Hopefulness and a promise of something untouchable hung in the air, and I always thought to myself that *nothing bad could happen—because it was Christmas . . .*

On the twenty-fourth of December, just one day after your birthday, the brink of Christmas Eve evoked tingles of anticipation in our stomachs as the hours moved further into the night, and tucked beneath the sheets snug in our holiday jammies, we barely touched the depths of slumber. Finally, the dark, still hours of morning would approach, and my eyes would begin to flutter, adjusting to the blurred numbers on the clock that sat atop my old, antique dresser.

With instantaneous, untouched realization, my eyes would open wide. "TOEY!" I would whisper, turning to you. "It's Christmas!" Being the only morning of the year when you woke up willingly, I'd wait in enthusiasm, as I watched you shake from your inner dreamland, and jostle yourself excitedly awake.

Quietly, we would emerge from my bedroom and venture toward the stairway banister lovingly decorated by Mom as we huddled together within the stillness of the house, tiptoeing in the untouched mystery of something undiscovered, whispering promises into the silent, Christmas morning air. Giddy, we linked our arms closely together, and peaked our eyes slowly down to the world, below . . .

The smell of fresh pine and holiday-scented candles perfumed through the fir- and ribbon-covered garlands along the banister. Everything waited in awe and wonder.

Eagerly examining every aspect of the house with new eyes, our dancing glances surveyed *what changes* lay in the rooms, below. Old, hand-knit stockings passed down from our great grandmother had once hung limply over the fireside and were now heavily weighted from upon the mantel as shapes of twisted ribbons and colors bloomed over the tops.

On a small, round, wooden table near the old antique arm-chair, a half-empty glass of milk sat beside cookie crumbs on a small, circular green-and-white plate.

The tree stood tall, both quiet and alive, with hanging silver tinsel surrounding ornaments that our family had carefully un-packed and hung in the weeks before, and it sparkled amid the tips of the branches of pines.

We weren't allowed to open anything without being together as a family, but we remained aware . . . that there were *new gifts under the tree.*

And leaning against the thick, timbered wood of the front door—"There!" I said, and pointed—

side by side, a single gift for each of us to unwrap

while Mom and Dad remained asleep upstairs.

The joy burst giddily between us in the holiday air as we ran down to surprises we couldn't wait to uncover.

After the tight-taped paper had been discarded and the ribbons unfolded, impatience for more would eventually ensue, and only a couple of short hours later, crawling back up the stairs like ex-cited puppies, we would shake Mom and Dad's feet from beneath their comforter as we begged them to wake and begin our Christ-mas morning together, as a family.

You sailed away with Dad to the San Juan Islands through the years he was alive.

You had your connection with him on the deck of that sail-boat, out on those great, open bodies of water.

Mom and I went along sometimes, too, and together, we stood atop our rocking sailboat, *Jasmine,* as it trailed the waters surrounded by the bouldering islands that arose from the Puget Sound.

Tidal changes and underpulls of what lay within our family's currents deepened beneath that vessel as we sailed through the years . . .

Most know, but so seldom want to acknowledge—that what is brewing beneath the surface can never be escaped. As we stand on deck beside the family we are born into and hope they will keep us afloat through the more vulnerable years of our lives.

It was spring but felt more like the tail end of winter, when you set out gliding on your first solo race along the waters of Lake Washington. You were ten, and Dad was far within his cancerous journey, moving past the points of failing battles, into a dying surrender with no return.

He'd just been released from the hospital that day, after another round of treatment to palliate more than mend his prognosis.

The water on the lake was stormy, and the air, cool and gray. All alone inside on your little *opti* you sat shivering beneath the gray, clouded, hovering sky that mirrored the unaffectionate waves, sloshing and jostling your little sailboat harshly in the wind.

I don't know what was going on for Dad. Maybe he was upset about the diminishing success of his efforts to survive, or maybe he simply didn't feel good. But beneath what was never named, an anger emerged from him that day that felt like the long-overdue ruins of old hurt, debts of rage that came up for air from some buried place deep within, where they had hidden, harbored for decades before . . .

In all his unawareness, the anger that day was directed at you . . .

You and Dad had collided in your differences, despite your shared love of sailing. Your varying personalities were marked: where Dad pushed, you needed to move slowly at your own pace, while he forged ahead with a certain determination, you needed to find your own timing and rhythm.

I watched from the stern of a family friend's boat—you, out on the water in your race, and Dad, as he leaned over the side, and *berated* you from the deck. Yelling at you, his jaw clenched and his face sickly white. "Goddamnit, Toey!" he growled, as you struggled at the stern.

Whatever you weren't "doing right," the palpability of his anger was felt within our boat across the waters, making its way to you, only causing you to shut further and further down. As you sat sinking into yourself and shivering, crying through uncertain tears in your boat on the lake.

You should know, whatever the anger was—*it wasn't about you.*

I've wondered, even years later, if you believed that it was.

I think Dad's life was coming apart, and in the undoing, he dispelled the remnants of his rage toward you.

You didn't deserve it . . .

Shivering while you jostled in choppy waters, sitting inside the little hull, a ball of chubby boy scared in a boat of choking sobs, tears flowing aboard the rain-slicked deck, your life jacket creeping up to your ears . . .

Few children can function under the heaviness of a dying parent—blazing at them amid a lonely storm.

You tried to sail that tiny vessel in the harsh and violent waves of the lake alongside what should have been the support of a sturdier, larger boat nearby.

Dad died that November.

The people who had frequented our home and lives during the months before trailed swiftly away, and we were mostly left alone.

A house can have so much movement when a person is dying, and as the months stretch on top of each other, it's easy to assume someone will always be there.

What a shock to the system—to discover their presence is simply a revolving around the dying.

And then, the house becomes sparse and bare, and the people in it are left behind . . .

Mom receded, and the phone calls stopped coming.

I tried to tuck you in at night, make sure you'd had something to eat. Knocking on your door, I said, "Hey Toe, did you have your dinner?"

You didn't want me—and lay curled away in the hunched figure of a ball.

I don't remember much of you from that time . . .

You were only ten years old.

That was when the years began to change.

Within you. Within me.

Between us both.

What followed Dad's dying was loneliness in our house, perhaps more marked than the whispers from the years before. The friends from families we once knew were gone, and the magic of the holidays lost their sparkle, even when Mom tried so hard to keep the sparkle going . . .

It didn't matter when she met someone two months later. We were relieved to see her off the floor. Together, she and the new guy whisked quickly off into their own world, which seldom had to do with ours.

Where you and I once rolled and shouted from ditches and played, watching movies together in the dusk of day, now you were distanced and far away. Even when you were near. Deep inside the enclave of your room, right next door to mine.

No matter the proximity, inside, you were farther, still.

The sailboat wallpaper that lined the walls of your bedroom was now covered by dark posters of heavy metal bands. *Korn. Limp Biscuit. Tool.* I knocked, and opened the door to a room that was dark despite the afternoon sun. Blinds closed, a smell, dense, like unaired, pre-adolescent boy.

I leaned against your wall and knocked my knuckles again. "Whatcha doin'?"

You were hunched over your desk facing away from me.

"Huh? Nothing . . ." you murmured, not looking back.

I stood, waiting. Wondering what to do or say. Bass and drums played on the speakers, distracting the silence beneath.

Most of my attempts to connect in those days somehow failed. Trying to convey some warmth or normalcy in contrast to the fallout of the life downstairs, in the house below.

I felt the lack.

And sighed, closing the door behind me.

It would be another year until I would begin to understand how your withdrawal was connected to some hidden hole of an escape that you'd found inside.

Once in a while, there were still moments when we found our way back into the sibling rhythms we had once had.

When Mom would cook, which wasn't often anymore, we still had to do the dishes. Standing at the sink, washing—I would soap-and-rinse, and you would dry.

A subtle poke of an elbow would progress into a more deliberate and teasing shove, and nudging each other with pretend annoyance, the water continuing to run as soapsuds bubbled and burst.

Out of nowhere, the sound of a *slap* would fill the kitchen, and you would cry, "Ouch! Sissy!!!"

Now, let's be honest—since we both know the truth: both of my hands were wet and soapy as they clung to dishes in the sink. And so, *unable* to hit you, I narrowed my eyes and glanced sideways at you from where I stood beside you at the counter.

You looked right at me, grinned, and—*slap*—did it again.

"Ouch!" you yelled. I stood, glaring. "Stop it. That hurts," you laughed, sardonically, in a lower tone.

Our eyes locked, I tried not to laugh as I bit the inside of my lower lip to maintain the exterior of annoyance. And then, we waited.

On cue, Mom's voice came shouting through the news on the TV in the den—

"Anna! You leave him alone!"

You grinned, the satisfaction of rivalrous contentment, and I whined my defense through the walls of the kitchen toward the living room. "I didn't do anything!"

Slap.

"Ouch," you murmured, laughing, interrupting my plea.

"Anna! Stop it!"

I squinted at you, shaking my head, jaw clenched but halfway smiling, and splashed water from the sink onto your oversized, blue-striped shirt, as I watched you dart away, trying to snap me with the kitchen towel.

"I'm going to fucking get you, Toey," I warned, ready to return the favor with more water in hand.

"Oh yeah? Come and get it, Sis."

Laughing and whining as the wet towel hit my leg, soapsuds filled the air, Mom fake-reprimanded us from the other room, and

I marveled in the false façade of annoyance and genuine delight of it all . . .

Behind those small moments, so much of you remained out of view as you rescinded behind the years of adolescence. Most of what I came to know of you existed only as rhythms of movements around me rather than connection itself.

When I couldn't hear your skateboard slamming onto the pavement in irritating redundance as you practiced ollies and kick-flips in the driveway, your techno music blared from behind the walls of your bedroom adjacent to mine. Sitting at my desk doing homework, I would roll my eyes and let out an exasperated "Uuggghhhh," before slamming my hand on the wall to get you to quiet down. "Toey! Your music is too loud! Shut up! I'm studying!"

You would turn the dial down a single, barely audible notch, and the *dum dum dum* would continue blaring through the walls.

In the evenings, I could hear you outside my bedroom door as you tripped in your oversized jeans on the stairway, coming back upstairs from getting a snack in the dead of night. *"Doh. Ouch..."* you'd murmur, after the *thud* rattled the floor.

Your jeans were always too long, dragging over your feet . . .

Also, you were stoned.

One night around eleven o'clock, I thought I heard a creak on the floor of my room while I was asleep and lying with my head turned away from the door, facing the windows.

I was in high school, and my desire to move away from our family had begun manifesting in my surroundings, as I pretended my room was a tiny New York studio apartment and mentally constructed a small inner architecture that kept me separate from the house below. I closed the bedroom door to keep my haven fresh with air from open windows and began collecting small pieces of furniture for when I moved away, which I dreamed of nightly as I infused my sleep with images of living far across the country.

A twelve-pack of Coke was kept in my room as part of the assembly of my "studio" retrieve, and you knew I kept one at the foot of my bed.

As I began to register the sound in the room from a place far within my slumber, I slowly opened my heavy eyes to discern what might be moving within the room.

But all I heard was silence, and so I quickly drooped back down toward sleep.

Just as I began to succumb to the consciousness of dreams, *there it was again—*

a small, strange sound.

I opened my eyes wide, sat up in bed, and looked around the room, just as I registered the gentle sound of a Coke can resettling inside the cardboard box down on the floor.

As my eyes adjusted in the night, I also saw that my bedroom door was slightly ajar . . .

"Toey?!" I sprang from my sheets and crawled over the foot of the bed to the frame.

Down on the carpet, flat on the floor in an army crawl, was you, lying face down. Frozen and caught in the act, you looked up with one of my Cokes in your hand.

"Yeah???"

Your presence those years might have been growing more obscure, but even in the hiding, I could still sense the humor in your skillful labor of laziness all the same . . .

High school continued, and when I wasn't away at one of my best friends' houses, or rehearsing for a play after school, we crossed paths in the kitchen sometimes, usually late at night.

The microwave would beep as it opened and you slid a plate with a soft taco made from flour tortillas, cheese, and that red *La Victoria* salsa from the fridge.

"Hey, make me one, too?" I'd say, just so that I could have some time with you, even when I wasn't hungry.

"Here, Sis." You'd plop an extra tortilla in the microwave, as I mashed an avocado to guacamole inside a small bowl, and the legs of the kitchen chairs would scratch the wooden floor as we pulled them from beneath the table. We'd sit across from each other, just as we had when we were little kids, when you clumsily spilled glasses of milk, except now we ate tacos, as our eyes stared down at the subtle indentations of time wearing itself into the grain of our antique kitchen table.

I'd look up at you, try to get a conversation started, and ask how things were going, but swallowing the rest of your taco whole, you'd briefly respond—"fine"—and then swiftly scoot your chair back out and stand to place your dish in the sink.

"Night, Sissy," you'd say—as you disappeared around the corner.

I replied to an empty room "Night . . ."

In the quiet disappointment of the downstairs of the house, the clicking of Mom's antique clock swished from where it hung on the wall. I would stand to turn out the lights that had been left on, close the garage and lock the doors, and walk back up to my enclave adjacent to your closed and impenetrable door.

ᑐ

In spring of my junior year of high school, you and I found ourselves standing outside on the driveway together one evening. It was just after the clocks had wound "spring ahead," and the hours were beginning to find relief as they further lengthened with light. The evening was warm despite gray skies, and I had just come home from a play rehearsal, and run outside in my sweats and socks to grab something from the car.

It was by chance that we crossed paths. I barely saw you at all anymore, but I'd begun to understand that you were using drugs more and more through the vague whispers of your friends, and some hunch I couldn't dislodge from the center of my spirit. Besides the pungent smell I sometimes detected outside my bedroom window, the remaining picture was slowly piecing together from the clues you dropped from time to time, and I sensed your drug use spread further and deeper than the hash whose smoke rose from the ground outside.

We started talking about something and I saw your eyes were swollen and sunken inward. Still, paradoxically, some conversation flowed between us in a way that it hadn't for a while, and I felt our streams connect into an echo of what we'd once had, and sensed in the settled gathering of my body, how I missed our kind of relating.

Sensing an estuary through the small, opening moment, I casually motioned the conversation toward drugs, and the extent of what you were involved in began taking greater shape. A newfound candidness from you poured between us, as I heard the words "oxycontin" and "ecstasy," and an urgent anger began burning beneath my terror, as my own unmetabolized experience around loss and dying conglomerated into a fiery pit in the center of my stomach.

Bluntly, I forged words from the bottommost place of honesty which I doubted anyone around us, in their casualness, self-absorption, and dismissiveness, had the courage to say.

"You could die."

The words hung in the fresh, spring air between us and a bird sung somewhere from the trees. After a moment of reprieve, as the forthright intonations left my gut and passed with an ache through my body, angered sadness further erupted within my chest. Sensing I could lose my grasp on you at any second, and not knowing where you would fall, as images of finding you over-dosed and dying flashed from a repeated script I'd been playing again and again in my mind through the years, the rage brimmed tearfully from my eyes, and I screamed.

"You're barely alive!!!"

Panic I could only feel but not fully understand gripped around my heart as a frenzied, electric charge shot throughout my mind and I stared straight into you, and then waited.

My lower lip began to tremble. My hands sequestered into small, clenching fists I held close to my body.

So much grief had gone unspoken in our home, and for so long, I'd felt I didn't know what to do as the years had passed by and you continued to slip farther out of reach. Now, standing to-gether along the plains of what was real, a sudden feeling of sickness flowed inside me as my mind raced to accept what now hung in the space between us.

You listened and looked down at the driveway.

You paused, and then quietly said—

"I know, Sissy . . ."

I stood, my eyes agape, not knowing what to do, and the bird's song fell into a sullen tone between the branches.

And then, you walked away.

I thought I could see a tear running down your face as the dragging sound of your slippers scuffed across the garage floor, and the antique doorknob of the backdoor turned, and you shut the door softly behind you.

I stood for a moment alone in the driveway, upset and uncertain in my socks atop the pavement.

Then, a strange calmness settled in the air, like the ions that usher a charge into the sky in the moments just before a thunderstorm.

Loneliness poured through me, and I wanted you to come back again.

From the corner of my eye, the red of Dad's old Saab sat collecting green mildew over the exterior. I glanced, and then drifted my gaze across the backyard, beyond the fence over the grass to the old oak tree that we'd hidden behind as we'd played with our best friends next door only a few, short years before—

only a moment ago.

For two years, a hand-drawn five- and ten-year calendar hung pinned on the wall above my desk.

I started researching graduate schools on the East Coast when I was sixteen so that I could move toward a life I imagined would be far different from the one I was living at home.

After a brief flirtation with musical theater, I decided on the practical course of becoming a physician's assistant. I researched the ins and outs of various specialties, contacted programs, and interviewed people in the field. Specific notes of what I would need to get into school hung beside the calendars that carefully outlined the safety of my future:

Four-year college degree—

    prerequisite coursework—biology, microbiology, chemistry, anatomy, and physiology—

two years of direct patient contact, plus volunteer work (note: call
nearby hospital) . . .

I researched the certifications I could complete to gain my
clinical experience and moved out when I was eighteen to live in
an apartment in the city. I got a job working in oncology and continued the college courses I had begun during my last two years
of high school.

By the time I was twenty-two, I was about to complete my
undergraduate degree and finally ready to prepare my long-sought
applications for graduate school. Excitedly, I collected my letters
of recommendation, tallied the accumulation of my clinical hours,
and prepared to finish my final classes to graduate in the spring.

It was Mom who called from the hospital, hysterical, saying that
you had overdosed after consuming eight hundred and fifty mil-
ligrams of oxycontin.

I couldn't register much of the drive to the emergency room,
but I remember standing in the ER with you on the gurney across
from Mom and our previous stepdad, whom she had brought
along. Married those short months after Dad had died, then divorced, remarried, divorced, and now back together again, here
they were, "sober now," standing by the bed of your collapse. I
breathed through my discomfort and irritability as I sensed the
dynamic between the three of us, and we watched you move in
and out of consciousness. I was angry at the invasion. His presence, I knew, would only accentuate the inconsistencies of what
I suspected would be Mom's short-lived performance at compe-
tent parenting and one she would play off at your expense.

Over the next few hours, it became clear that you needed treatment, but we would soon discover that apparently the quantity of

drugs you had been using was so high that you wouldn't qualify for a state-funded detox facility.

"We're sorry, but these facilities just don't have the resources to deal with extreme withdrawal symptoms," the social worker said, and then left the room.

I was irate, but remained calm, as I absorbed the reality that you would have to detox on your own, without any professional help or guidance, with no one in that hospital room knowing what to do. My mind began tracing the practical steps of what would need to come next.

I believed at the time that rehab was the unnamed necessity in the equation. But I didn't even bother to ask if that's what you wanted or felt you needed.

I just looked at you crumbled into a ball, and assumed signing you into rehab was what needed to be done.

When the social worker left the room, Mom and our former stepdad claimed somewhat unnaturally in front of the hospital staff that came to hand over your discharge papers that they would take you home to "get you clean."

I felt the bind—finishing my last quarter in school and knowing I wouldn't be able to complete my classes with the simultaneous role of taking care of you. And even though I knew in my gut their proclamation of support for you wouldn't last, I didn't know what else to do.

And so, I let you go home with them, back to where so much of this problem originated.

Knowing, as soon as I walked out of that hospital, they'd never see the rehabilitation through . . .

The next day, the phone rang—Mom was "falling apart" from the stress of it all.

I drove the forty-five minute drive to pick you up, gathered your things inside the confines of my car, and brought you home to where I lived above the waters of the arboretum in the city.

Ten years of chronic drug use beginning when you were ten years old, from marijuana, to ecstasy, to oxycontin, took a toll on your spirit, and the toxic discharge sloshed within remnants of too many unmet needs stacked on top of layers upon layers of undigested harm. Ejected through your body, soul, and mind, agonizing, aching waves of pain reverberated through hair-drenched fevers, and you had little ability to come up for air, or find respite from what was being discharged, as you dropped to the ground.

Even though I'd been working in the hospital the last couple of years, I didn't know what I was doing when it came to detoxing you, only what signs to look for if I needed to take you back—to the structure that was supposed to help but had left us to suss through fevering waves of sorrowful, bile-filled pain alone: *Unbreakable fever, too much vomiting. Shaking and tremors are different than seizures—could this happen, too?* I researched and kept an eye on you as I found my footing with you, day by day.

I pulled open the sofa bed inside the small study with the window overlooking the lily-padded waters of the arboretum below, and the springs that crunched beneath the cushions unfolded from themselves. I made your "room" by removing old pictures of our family from the closed closet doors, and arranged them to face you on the bed, thinking that maybe if you were surrounded by the memories of the more supportive love we'd once had, it might provide some compensatory comfort or relief.

I know I was hoping to guide you as well in a return to what I believed was the source of your wounding—and that this plummet down to your rock bottom would somehow bring you closer to the open gash that needed to be healed.

I didn't have the best timing, then—

and lacked an understanding of the way people need to find their own paths to healing . . .

Protective barriers often took a back seat to the urgency I felt to work more closely with the origins of harm in my own self.

I tried desperately to excavate what I felt stood between us— even when that wall wasn't yet ready to be faced . . .

Those days passed, long, and sickly, and tired.

In the middle hours of the afternoon, when you could no longer turn to find a more comfortable position from where you rested, and the small, momentary opening of the fresh morning had long since worn off into the haze of day, I took you for short drives down to the water by the beach, hoping the fresh air and waves might clean away some of what felt so sickly and untouched.

Wondering, if maybe, seeing those boats out on the water might help you, too.

When we returned one day at the end of that first week and you went to lie back down, I watched you sleeping in the quiet hours of the early evening. The sun had begun to stretch its rays and dipped through the windows onto your bed on the pullout sofa where you were in a deep place of sleep, perspiring. Sweat sleeked strands of your brown hair to your face.

I wanted to move the damp hairs away, but left you alone.

Leaning in the doorframe, I watched your body rise and fall within each slow breath. You were curled inward on the small pullout twin bed, all six feet of you. The mattress sunk from your weight, with metal brackets supporting you on the floor. When had you become so tall and burdened with gray-like lead? I had missed your development into becoming a young man of nineteen, when I'd left the sparsity of that final season of adolescence together, four years ago.

How did we get here?

I wondered if I could determine the single point in time and put my finger where the wound lay, so I could discern its many layers and know what to do.

My mind wandered beneath the golden sun, setting with shadows moving over you and onto the floor, recollecting undefined moments, from people to circumstances throughout the years, layered together inside some truth hidden within an unseen magnitude, too much to understand in a single setting or word. So many years toppled on top of each other, with so many circumstances of harm: complex interchanges of abandonment and negligent, aching movements . . . and so much more I still didn't know. The images remained undefined and dragged together in a single, long stretch of dismissiveness in pain . . .

For a moment, my heart longed for things to feel alright again, the way I believed they had when we were little.

But then, I wondered, how much of that sense of youthful alrigthness was even true . . .

Anger brewed toward the disruptions. Images of our stepfather raging fed my own upset as I remembered him bellowing at you in random intervals like some sergeant figure attempting an authority he would never fulfill or have the capacity for. The flood turned toward Mom and the way she had gotten stoned with you over the years, recruiting you for her own supply. While you were still a teenager. Still a kid. Using. Heading toward here.

The eve of my high school graduation flashed, when you confessed to me that you had taken nine hits of ecstasy at a rave a few nights before. When I didn't know what to do I told Mom, said you needed help. She confronted you, yelled. You broke down, felt I betrayed you. And then, nothing happened. You all showed up to my graduation.

"You're ruining this for me," Mom had said, when I wouldn't slip into performative joy to fit the occasion.

You distanced yourself from me even more after that. And I wondered now if I should have known a better way to help you. You were fifteen.

I reflected on all the things that had taken us away from each other through the years, like the end of a string, fraying at the strands: no longer together, no longer connected. And I began to feel the pain of my own abandonments and then a guilt of feeling that I, too, had left you. You stayed home when I decided to leave. And when you did move out a few years later, I'm not sure you really took yourself with you.

Is there a fated number of inner resources each of us has to either press us further forward or take us down against whatever obstacles we all eventually must face?

What is the line between choice and helplessness?

I wondered why some people seemed to find a way out of harsh circumstances toward a better life, while others declined steadily, hidden behind harbors of quiet suffering, where they slowly spiraled into sunken levels of despair, like ghosts in the shadows motioning on a wheel that never stops turning, despite what I angrily felt was the opportunity to step off that wheel at any time . . .

The many indications we give each other, subtle but seeking, to convey we are drowning. Vocal intonations that are slightly off-key, rigid or overly laxed gestures of the body that indicate our false portrayals of the real worlds, below.

"How are you?"

"*I'm fine!*" The forehead lifts as eyes divert toward a disconnected gaze, the voice raising an octave higher than the resonance of natural tone.

We tell each other about our false compensations without ever really saying it.

I wondered if I should have pressed further, done more, tried asking about your music more often.

Didn't I try?

"It's going well."

The stone wall. There was nothing more you would give me . . .

I hit the barricade with my hands, and eventually, just walked away.

The sparseness, through all those years leading up to that moment together—when I was twenty-two and you were nineteen— and I hadn't been able to get any further with you, and there was nothing more you would allow me to see.

The warm spring blew through the small window screen, and I smelled the still water from the moorage beneath. And a sadness, a descent of rage that still lingers today from time to time— of watching you suffer and try to survive, and the way that I could neither seem to help or understand . . .

You wouldn't look at me on the morning when we drove to rehab.

I woke you up, sluggish and defeated, gently whispered, as my hand rubbed the side of your leg—"Hey, we have to go."

You were lying on your side, facing away from me, and wouldn't say anything.

Feet scuffed on the pavement on our way to the car in the open-covered parking lot of the building—

and then miles stretched beneath the tires on the highway that led us toward another part of the state.

Calm and quiet, I felt some subtle relief. Hoping others could help you through what I couldn't provide. I'd dropped my classes that term, unable to keep up during your detox, but beyond the immediacy in those early days of withdrawal, I didn't know what to do.

Tall evergreens, maples, and cottonwoods faded behind us as we drove into open and arid terrain, where gold grasses rolled over the hillsides, and dry, jagged gorges of rock dropped alongside the winding road toward the rehab center.

You smoked cigarette after cigarette, and the smoke blew hot from the air outside, sucked back into the car through the open windows, fumigating the space between us, as your gaze remained locked on the road, and I could feel you suffering.

Small, childlike helplessness and fragility seemed to erupt into the emotional desert between us. I looked at you from the corner of my eye, wanting to hug you, make it all better, keep you safe from all you were facing in that ripe, open tear of vulnerable terrain. But all I could do was tighten my hands around the black leather of the steering wheel, put my hand on your shoulder from time to time, and keep my eyes on the cracked road in front of me.

I slowed to a gentle stop, when three-and-a-half hours later, my car turned at a sign onto a rocky gravel road.

I silently turned off the engine, and we sat in a heavy, saddening quiet. Outside, the low hum of bugs buzzed, as they flew through the air.

You glanced toward me with heavy, half-closed eyes—defeated and afraid. And then, slowly lowered your head, as it fell into your hand.

A youthful version of you imploded in the car as you began sobbing, blurring the lines of what I thought I knew I should do, and opposing responses tugged within me, and for a moment, I didn't know what to do.

I blinked.

Keep it together, keep it together. Fall apart on the drive home. Fuck. Fuck, fuck, fuck . . .

Finding the force to be strong and loving made the moment seem as if "right" responses resided on one side of some thick, unchartered line. You kept crying, succumbing to fearful sobs, as tears welled and rolled through your exhausted, tired eyes and covered your face, dripping onto your shirt and down your neck, and you let them fall without wiping them away.

I put my hand on your back, sweaty and choking with fear, and rubbed it gently. "Alright, Toe," I said softly, "Let's get your stuff."

You choked again, and I felt you succumb to another uncontrollable sob.

"You know, it's only two weeks, and I'm going to come to see you this weekend, which is only a few days away, and you can call me whenever you need to, and I'll answer."

Do you hate me?

More silence.

"I know this is hard and that you're scared, but you're going to be alright, Toe Toe." My hand remained on your back as I tried to confer that I was still near, even though we were distancing, and you were embarking toward a turn in the road I could not follow.

When I leaned in and hugged you, I felt your sweating body gasp with tears from under my arms.

Then, pulling away, I ran my fingers over your hair as I looked at you, and you stared down into your lap. The shame and fear were palpable.

I turned and got out of the car.

I pulled your bag out of the back trunk and opened your door.

"Come on," I said.

Trying to crack a gentle smile, pulling my own tears back inside, telling myself that "this was the right thing to do." It was all I could muster. I was convinced the only way for things to be okay was to get you inside. There was nowhere else to drive to, no turn I could take, no one to call, and no body of water that could wash away the salt of your tears.

You slugged out of the car, dragging your feet . . .

Inside the rehab center, one of the staff took your bag and asked you to follow him to your room. Your voice raised slightly to a polite tone. Always respectful to strangers, even in your worst moment.

"Okay," you replied.

You turned and hugged me.

"I love you," I said, "and I'll see you soon."

"Yeah. Love you, too . . ." A barely audible whisper.

And then you turned and walked away.

I wept the whole drive home.

When the next weekend approached, just as I was preparing to step into the car for another journey back toward you, the phone rang.

It was Mom.

"We decided to pick your brother up yesterday," she said.
"He called, crying, and didn't want to be there."

∽

I moved to Paris a few months later in the fall and didn't see or hear very much from you for a while after that.

I returned to the Northwest later that year, and our silence was followed by more longstanding years of blank connection between us.

I would reach out, and maybe you would respond. A one- or two-phrase exchange.

You said you'd stopped using after the scare of your overdose, and met a girl whose love helped keep you tied to a different line. Your life slowly but surely bettered, from what I could discern, through a distant fog, very far away.

The few times we saw each other, we still watched movies, or ate in brief conversation. What visits there were were short and far between.

And then, more time would pass, and there would be nothing.

∽

For years, I wondered, when I reached and didn't hear back from you, what would become of our relationship, *if I were to stop reaching altogether?*

I met rage, feeling like the only lifeline toward a connection too far apart to hold.

And I still wonder what it is that makes us come apart when we were once so close together.

Something happens between us that we don't want to think about or say aloud—

but is it the circumstances that carry us apart, or ourselves?

Seeing a face from the place we come from can be a reminder of the things we long to forget.

Even though we may move differently through our lives, with personalities of our own—

this doesn't need to dampen our bond as brother and sister.

And we don't have to grow away from each other, even if we do not grow the same.

Today, we walk down a dirt path through the forest behind my house, with your dog scampering through the brush.

There's only one person in the world who fully knows where I come from.

And that person is you.

We revisit the memories of our younger days as we swirl spaghetti onto our spoons over my wooden kitchen table by the window—and together, we understand the joys and losses of our childhood, in ways no one else can.

No matter how close the ties of other friendships, or how intricately we retell the stories to new bonds we form in love—

between the racing fears, youthful excitements, and the inaudible fading of all that will never return,

no one will ever know the changing pulse of our home growing up—the way siblings do, like you and me.

Only you know Mom, and only you knew Dad, and our stepdad, in the incredible palpable recollections that infuse the memories of our story with realness.

Sitting across from you at the table tonight, pieces of spilled parmesan sprinkled atop the maple, I find comfort in our time together, whatever it may mean—

and however long it may last . . .

We laugh, as you give me tips on how to better cook pasta from your chef days in Italian kitchens, and I listen to your cumulative knowledge—the pride you take in what you have learned and become.

Somewhere, our closeness still lingers. And in a not-so-distant memory, I can still feel the way it was—

when our two bedrooms were adjacent—

when we crossed paths in the kitchen below—

and I could hear the *thump thump* of your music from the other side of my country wallpaper.

Then, an ache arises inside for a moment, in wondering—

why what we have always has to move on . . .

Your tires crunch the gravel driveway as you leave my house to return to a life of your own. The comfort of you stays with me as I settle back into my own rhythm—grateful, even in parting,

that though I know we don't have everything together—

or perhaps, maybe even a lot—

somewhere between us,

I know we still have something . . .

Feels Like Home

The pale blue house was surrounded by acres of farmland at the end of a dead-end road.

When I arrived at the island dock in the spring, it took a moment for the ferry to settle, and we rocked as the large vessel swayed gently in the water within the buoy rails. Waterfowl sprawled and then settled their wings, perched on the rise and fall of the wooden pier. I watched one loosen his stretching neck and twist it below the under-segment of his wing, catching the sky from his underbelly before erecting again to stand watch over the harbor. Over the rail of the ferry, down in the shallow waters, smoothly rounded rocks appeared to move through the gentle rise and fall of waves as the sun warmed the surrounding harbor. Shades of green were dispersed in rays of light that passed through small, rolling swells, illuminating quiet depths beneath the surface of the Puget Sound.

I heard the car clank as I rolled over the offramp, and soon was driving through acres of fields and long stretches of uncut grass, the sunlight wide in the early day of spring. Homes were perched amid the open and green land, grazed by the nibbling mouths of soft, white goats, as they wandered the pastures surrounded by thick, sturdy trunks of old ascending trees.

I signed the rental document with a dull ballpoint pen, took the keys, and shook the man's hand.

Then stood for a moment to breathe the clean, damp earth.

When I finally went to cross the threshold of the front door with the remainder of my belongings two weeks later, I paused, and remembered for a moment what I was leaving behind. My hand rested gently over peeling white paint on the frame of the door, and I wearily closed my eyes. Winter had taken away outworn parts of me through a slow, unfolding, tectonic shift. In the month's release of nauseating metamorphosis, I purged and tore back new layers of old problems—outdated to cope with the gaps of what I believed I needed, but still didn't have. The release those months dropped me toward were followed by long, stretching hours of silent aloneness in an apartment's dim afternoon light.

Perhaps we are given what we can handle. While many of those winter nights drudged forth a heavy dread that emerged through a descended and neglected part of my core, for a few short months that seemed to stretch into one long, ongoing ache that for a time I wasn't sure would end—throughout the weight of heavy water—my appreciation for the necessity of the long dark remained intact. A reverence and respect for the understanding: that through various times of change, pieces of who we are must emanate, ache, and then, let go.

Aspects of ourselves are born into a certain life cycle, and then must eventually decompose back into the humus of our interiority. I wandered in wintertime in the darkened aftermath of those deaths as literal and metaphysical pieces of my life crumbled away, leaving me with a space for an unsatiated taste of something sensed but still untouched.

The day I arrived at my new front door, antique and chipped and beautiful, I hoped that with some surrender, what had been let go would eventually receive a dose of transformation that could someday nourish something needed but not yet known.

I believed that what I'd left behind would open space in the world above . . . even though, aside from my young magpie cat, and the psychology classes I'd begun teaching at the university— there was still not a sprout of life to replace the blank, empty space.

Newness cannot be planted too soon, hushed in a hurry, just to avoid the open, aching plains of what's been blown away.

Light has a way of rising on a time all its own.

ᛉ

By the end of May, I sat on the front steps of that old farmhouse, watching the hydrangeas bloom, while joking to a friend on the phone one afternoon.

"It sort of seems like I'm sitting in this place where I've been wanting to be for so long—and it's just me and the grass." We laughed, and continued sharing in the ongoing, unfinished details of each other's lives, just as we had been doing in the years before.

Inside the house, I looked out through one-hundred-twenty-year-old window frames to the plentitude of earth that grew in the backyard. Long, uncut grass continued to grow beneath overgrown branches that weighed down, perhaps from being unattended in the seasons before, and the thorns of a blackberry bush were expanding as they climbed adhesively along the side of the house. Inside, the window shades were filled with a thick layer of dust, and the carpet had a wet, dirty tang of odor. Air in the heating vent smelled stale as it blew thick heat with particles of dust I soon discovered were remnants of never having been cleaned. The shelves along the staircase hall were broken and chipped off, and the chimney from the old wood-burning stove was black and coated with soot.

In and outside of the house, work needed to be done. But just beyond the door, the grasses seemed to grow faithfully—steady, calm, and serene.

I wondered, as I made a list of things to do, if what we leave unattended in our lives stems from our lack of strength in a moment—or a deflation of courage, and an unreadiness to confront what needs to go. I considered my own residual overgrowth of what I'd recently trimmed away as I traced my finger along the loose molding on a wall, and felt anxious trepidation of not knowing what would come next, or how it would even arrive, as I tried to press the misaligned wood back into place.

All the ways my own fear had for so long prevented my own budding bloom.

A week later, early in the morning, a small thrush sat on a bush outside my windowsill. I watched as the bird's wings flittered with rapid movement, filtering water through the contours of its delicate feathers, as it emerged from a bath on the gutter of my roof.

I rubbed my eyes as I sat on a bench by the window and thought of the way water trickles to places the eyes cannot always go. That in the pull of gravity lies a force to follow the unseen. I tried sensing what my life might be moving toward in this unknown place of becoming and thought of how long I had been wanting to live on the quiet of rural land, believing something in the slower life pace and open space would relieve what felt too constricted to open fully inside.

I'd left the city after a fifteen-year stay, and as I rid myself of old furniture, I held on to the meaningful keepsakes—my closest friends, resonating books, old sweaters. Teaching at the university was a significant cultivation of many years of work, study and dreaming that had just begun, and now branched into its own single, fresh new vine. My spunky cat, Lucy, was a presence of comfort as she ran through the open rooms of the unfilled space in process of becoming our home, hopping into recently unpacked, open cardboard boxes left in the kitchen after the move.

An echo of a relationship I believed would turn into marriage gone by, my newly discarded methods for filling the time, and the growing distances with certain friends as they walked new paths whispered from my periphery.

I gazed out the window, wanting to gain hopeful images of possibilities I could not yet clearly discern of what would come next as they hovered in the air above my view. For a long time, I continued to look with the same intense gaze I had carried throughout most of my life, as I watched neighbors from the houses nearby stroll by on their morning walks and wave.

The visions of what might be never came fully into view, and when the morning bird completed its cleansing baptism, it sat for a moment on a branch, and then flew away.

Time passed, and my tea had grown cold as the light shifted into stretching hours of the morning. I looked at a stack of books on the end of the bench where I was still seated—a used astrology reference sat over a text on psychoanalytic perspectives, with Celtic mysticism and a collection of poetry lying calmly near the bottom, reminding me of the necessary and limiting considerations of the symbolic. I'd been born in-between two astrological signs, the "cusp of rebirth"—just after winter had passed into spring—and I thought of my ongoing framework toward life-death cycles and the apparent affinity I held for liminal spaces. When I considered my actual birthing process, I hadn't been able to finish naturally on my own time, and had been cut out early instead, surrounded by the drowning fluids of anesthesia. I loosely traced my history of not landing for too long in any one place, relationship, or pursuit before I felt the need to continue moving forward, and wondered if that movement was at once a fear of dying, a reenactment of my own interrupted arrival, and itself a desire for authentic birth.

The psychoanalytic text sat heavily with its weight-filled and clearly defined reductionist perspectives, and I considered how my underlying ambivalence toward landing in a settled place might also reflect avoidance. Resistance to having and then losing what was dearest to me sent aching memories through my body, and for a moment, my father flickered in the periphery of my mind.

I'd struggled at times to complete things—degrees, books, creative ideas that never became tangible. Was this a natural process? In the end, I seemed to press through to finish the things that really mattered, but at thirty-three years old, I was beginning to recognize I didn't want to accumulate a collection of aborted cycles. It can be difficult to reach fully for various forms of life when you know death will follow. Completion is both an arrival and a death.

Perhaps I had believed unknowingly that by circumventing the full cultivation of various cycles and their joys, that I would also be spared further pain. I went to touch a speck of dust on the windowpane, and then left it on the wood, hoping that whatever my wounding and brokenness, some stubborn determination to live as fully as possible would soon be reflected in the tangibility of my surroundings—and that despite whatever hardships might inevitably follow, my attempt to stand firmly and surrender to the gifts and losses of the life I created would be enough.

I looked around the unpacked room and knew that being here was as much about slower rhythms and clean island air as it was about trying to actually land further within my life.

But something ineffable hovered within and around me, and I knew our interpretations need to hold room for more than what can spring from the alluring seduction of singular ideas.

Whatever insights I was now able to glean about myself, deeper truths probably lay somewhere within, between, beneath, and beyond whatever theories I was able to string together. The necessity for tolerating what still remains unknown as I sought to understand my own becoming incited a familiar feeling of impatience: for wanting to understand more fully the complexities about who we all are, answers that themselves never seemed to come full circle.

Across the road, I saw a neighbor's child hop along the grass, and a significant longing for greater simplicity that had stretched through the entirety of my life beat quietly inside my chest.

Beyond what I was able to compile about myself and my experiences in life up until that point—the stories, psychologies and spiritually infused beliefs—something I could sense, but didn't know where to place, remained—an elusiveness of knowing that would forever remain unformed.

Mystical overlaps with matter.

I stood, and began arranging books around the room, and then went outside to cut a few stems of flowers that lined the fence and place them inside the hollow opening of a tall, thin vase, where I set them beside the newly arranged and re-erected books.

I knew somewhere I'd always eventually stumble onto a faithful bud of blossom to burgeon my understanding—even if those meaningful frameworks were sometimes meant only for particular seasons.

Somewhere, I'd always reached joy again, like the opening that comes from the lengthening hours of daylight on the first days of spring.

And I was born just on the cusp of that new season of arrival.

Like soiled lavender, I could spring from the ground once more.

Rooted below—but blossoming in the sun.

The next day, I heard my tires crunch on the small gravel lot of an old white building five minutes from my house as I pulled in to park.

Inside, a dance studio sat quietly, soft air drifting through its open windows. Cedarwood bars in perfect straight lines were tightly secured to walls across from full-length mirrors, and the smell of marley flooring hovered subtly within the space. The large, open windows along the back of each room invited light from the outside, and its specks danced through the shining bright green leaves into the building, illuminating shadows on the floors.

A psychic woman once told me she saw me teaching dance classes to children. I'd met her by chance in passing, and something in her words resurrected an abandoned part of me. I danced as a young girl. Neglected memories of stretching over my tiny legs as I breathed and found comfort in the harbor of my focus began to emerge. After that conversation, I began, even just in my imagination, to feel a return to a part of my home, inside.

I'd been taking classes at the studio since I'd arrived, and as fate would infer, discovered one week after moving that there was a recent opening to teach classes to young kids. Now, in the middle of June, in the early sprawling light of afternoon, my eyes were following young dancers as they twirled in a kaleidoscope of colorful flowing scarves.

I watched their imaginations lead the way, and smiled, as I sat on my knees in the center of the room, a quiet joyfulness beginning to swell from somewhere deep inside. Light water began to form at my eyes, and I felt a slight longing echo that was not too far from the wells of unforgotten grief.

Their small faces squinched as they pressed through muscles to stretch their small, pointed toes, and the floor puttered with the sound of tiny feet before a momentary hovering silenced the air, and they leapt through the skies.

Children are inspired so freely by a life that shines from within.

I thought of the wondrous movement that can come from the unfiltered center of our innermost being, when we are allowed to emerge uninterrupted into a world that might actually long to hold and know us—

for who we really are.

What it means to be safe, I thought to myself—

and I watched them fly.

When the class finished, the room stood empty, the swift eruption of childlike energy gone like the breeze. Stagnant summer air held silent and hovering, and I began to remember how, when I was young, I used to do things more freely.

I was unusually flexible and thin-framed as a girl, and could lengthen and contract myself lyrically as I moved an inward song reaching out—

with no hesitation, guarding, or signs of wary vigilance.

And then, one day, I stopped.

It took many years for the ripples of that ceasing to take form in other shapes of my life, but they did. For a long time, what was once a fuller and more natural movement through the world became a life half-lived, half-hidden—

a *one foot in, one foot out*—

a dance all its own,

of never again really submerging

into fully desired waters.

I remained in-between worlds, in the years after the ground beneath me was lost. When my father died. My mother fell apart. My brother began to disappear. And what I believed I knew of myself was challenged on a scale I could not grasp or comprehend.

In never really reconciling those severances with enough meaning that could hold me through the years that followed, I had forgotten what it meant to move with fullness, freedom, and surrender—

just when I was learning the dance.

Over the coming months, I tepidly began retracing my abandoned steps within those studio walls. And I started, however slowly, to reconfigure inside of me what had been left behind.

With my eyes closed, I moved and remembered something that was never truly lost,

but still somehow long forgotten.

ᏻ

Stretching further into the weeds of summer, the hours of the day grew long. I ascended the stairs to the small attic one afternoon as they creaked, and the heat pressed up to meet me. I stacked one box of books on top of another, and began unpacking more gathered thoughts, feeling where to place the appropriate pages on the shelves I had just assembled tiredly the day before.

Inside one of the boxes, I pulled out a small journal, and paused. On the front of that cloth cover was a single evergreen tree, not unlike the ones that surrounded my house outside the window. Inside, the first page was dated 1999. My eighth-grade biology teacher had given me that journal in the beginning of winter just after my dad had died when I was just thirteen.

I stroked my hand over the soft cover and wondered if something in her spirit had sensed what I'd needed?

I closed the cover and leaned the small, dark green binding beside a dozen others I had filled through the years.

An echo of similar memory reminded me of the ways I had perhaps been seen *enough* by others whose help I hadn't believed I'd needed in the years when I was growing up. For a time that stretched from mid-adolescence into my early twenties, a particular life plan carried me on an overarching wave I rode to endure the chaos of my home life and uncertainty of what was to come. Believing I wanted to go into medicine, having researched everything I would need to get into school since I was sixteen, I believed I could get by without the help of people who didn't know me in order to get to where I was going.

The mind has a sophisticated way of avoiding disappointment.

Enter my undergraduate school psychology advisor when I was twenty. In a required appointment (which I didn't think I needed), I pulled out a list of planned coursework and outlines for everything that was required for me to complete graduate school applications, when she looked back at me and said— "Have you thought of becoming a teacher?"

Emotional incompetence and marred feedback from so many of the people in my early life hadn't helped blossom my faith in receiving clear pools of reflection from adults. But like the resonating words of the psychic who had envisioned me dancing with children, and like the journal my eighth-grade biology teacher had insisted I touch pen to paper on, something in my advisor also *knew*—and in her words, a chord was struck which reverberated back to some melody I'd had inside of me since the earliest beginnings of my life, but which had never found the validation or courage to come up for song.

Whatever confidence had been taken out of me in the howling years of shifting floorboards of my childhood, my father passing and my mother and brother in their ways falling away, had left true corners of my being hiding in quiet moors of murky doubt.

That advisor was the same woman who hired me to teach psychology the winter before—when all other outgrown paths were dying, and that one string of honest purpose kept me tethered when so much else seemed to be falling away.

In August, having befriended the farmer who tilled land in front of my house, I walked up and down rows between various assortments of greens. Mustards, kales, brussels sprouts, and cabbages lined the field, and I saw where thin, small lines of green sprouted garlic through the brown-laden earth. In her daily labor, I often watched from the distance of my front steps as I drank tea in the morning and she leaned down to place unopened seeds into a ground that could one day soon bring rise from various roots to harvest. I newly saw and thought of what back-bending work it was—actually growing things.

Apple, pear, and plum trees were ripening, and their own labors were beginning to fall to the ground. I walked the land around the periphery of where my house sat, sifting mentally through messages I had received throughout my life about what love really is.

I kept trying to consider, sort though, and then discard what didn't seem fit to remain planted inside.

And I remembered—having been afraid to love because I did not want to lose, and the way I had leaned into loved anyway, only to choose people who leave.

Relationships in all their various forms, were one thing I had sought to do well . . .

But as I walked that day in the shifting sun, I wasn't sure I'd cultivated as much fabric as my desire hoped for. With the long end of a piece of grass between my teeth, I fumbled with the recognition that while I was in some regards alone, there was an absence of regret for what I had felt I had to leave behind. And further still, part of me questioned, and wondered if perhaps being alone was also somehow my fault.

I knew my parents loved me, even if their love came in crooked forms sometimes—and in others, never came at all.

I had learned that sometimes, we love things that are not good for us—and over time, have to decide if we will let those people leave.

I remembered *the painter*, who asked me to marry him less than a decade ago. How much my spirit so easily embraced his love— and all the ways he had shown me both what I did and did not need. That through his face I had encountered the places of my own wounding.

The faces of those with other messages and lessons passed before my storyboard of memories. Whether I could have remained within certain arrangements so as not to be alone—but I also knew that I would have to become what I wasn't in order to be wanted in the shadowy mires of falser love.

The invitation is always available to overlook the abandonment that comes from forsaking ourself, in the hope of receiving what is supposed to be embracing, honest, and kind. Showing up fully without recoil; offering to hold and asking to be held in the ongoing expansion and contraction that is authentic living; and accepting with unutterable grief the places we may genuinely but unsuccessfully try to find one another, is something different than the bypassing that comes from the dismissive avoidance of what so many choose to not even try to see.

New stems of yarrow blew in the wind that lined the fence around my home, emerging from withered mulch that had wept wetly into the ground. I made my way back to the house, and looking across the property, considered what a resilient undertaking it was—to continue trying to cultivate new life, when much of what we hope for so often never comes to bloom.

I'd considered whether the journey was worth the risk and heartache, when confronting so much disappointment, in the face of what hadn't come through.

Coming alive again was something I'd always had to choose.

Perhaps love is various shades of knowing and being known—an acceptance of ourselves and others, alongside some longstanding enduring of uncertainty, never knowing the fullness of who we are—and all the while gaining some ability: to offer *clearly enough* the corners of truth that echo from every crevice of us inside, as we attempt to hold strong to ourselves and each other.

I had sensed those fragrances briefly, a few times . . .

I tossed the grass and went back inside the house, knowing that no person, teacher, or philosophy was going to determine what love was for me—even though those pages of books were scattered open around my living room, flapping openly in the breeze beneath some stone I had picked up on the road.

In the end,

> I would have to continue discerning what love was
> for myself.

The next morning, I woke early and went back into the farmer's garden at dawn. Steam rose from the ground with the rising light over the open rows of fresh-tilled dirt. Scents of the earth surfaced with the light—

> moist soils, waiting to embed whatever she would continue to drop, steadily,
>
> > through open fingers into the ground.

A few sunflowers sprawled themselves under the dew nearby, their vibrant yellow petals opening into the early rising light—

> and I wondered how much the love still within me,
>
> > might only be resting
> >
> > and asleep . . .

Two finches sat perched on the lichen-covered fence near decomposing thistles among the grass, and I turned to see a larger blue jay flutter through the branches nearby.

◯

Both of my grandmothers were gone now.

It was September, and I thought of my Grandma Uno on my mother's side, as I lightly traced the keys of the piano she'd left me when she died. She'd been nicknamed after the card game. After a long journey up winding roads of the West Coast, the piano was now at home within the walls of my living room. I touched the ivory, dragging my fingers along a crescendo of unplayed chords.

A memory of when I was young, singing through the open windows of my bedroom illuminated the air—but like the dancing I had forsaken, I, too, had for many years dropped that tune, unable to find my way back into songful harmony.

Behind me, my father's mother, framed in her black-and-white silhouette, smiled at me from her picture on the ledge.

The old wooden bench creaked as I sat early in the evening and began to hum something I'd never heard, as a sage leaf burning in a seashell made smoke that streamed a calm, mossy scent into the air that began to fill with melody, as I played and sang through open windows . . .

When the sky began to drop darker into shades of evening blue, I waved to one of the neighbors as he was walking down the road in front of the house.

"I heard you're a writer . . . You know this farmhouse has belonged to other writers. I think it has been waiting for you."

His words released an ache I could not pretend to utter or describe.

We said goodbye, and beneath a sky that was blowing the summer toward its dusk, I surrendered to that unmet need for belonging, and moved to the wicker chair in the corner of the room.

Words flowed from me as if they were always meant to come from some unopened place inside.

And, to make contact with that once still and open page.

When the words had had their say, cool blue and turquoise color still lined the thinly lit sky, and out on the open grass, eyes wet from remnant tears, I knelt, resting my knees on an earth damp with recent rain, and pressed my hand atop the cool soil before submerging my fingers into the moist ground.

When my hand rose, the dirt fell and sifted through my fingers. And I was changed.

⸹

In October, I stared through the glass sliding door of my study over the grass, whose growing patterns had become more familiar, and the wearing wood fence that lined the periphery around the backyard. The various rose bushes and lilac trees I had trimmed that summer were now beginning to turn shades of red, yellow, and brown. A mental collage of theoretical reflections and academic prompts for students was making its way to the notepad on my desk, and the ideas trailed with me as my eyes gazed out upon the turning leaves.

As the earth faced its autumn of life, pigmented changes emerged from the vibrant eruption of the falling. The once flourishing now floated slowly down and lay dying on wet ground, releasing implosions of color unlike any before the decay.

I admired the beauty.

Bare branches of maples and extending evergreens reached from the roots of trees that bore the leaves into being, and I abandoned my notes for a walk in the early chill of evening.

The island winds were like a symphony through the tips of surrendering branches that played and began to sway with my recollected memories. I wandered, wondering just where in time I had begun to hibernate the tenderest parts of myself that were now returning to take a proper place in the forefront of my life after so long retreating into the restful past—barricades away from the world.

In the open winds, I looked up to the dark green, where like the leaves above, we all come sprouting into the earth together, only to fall downward in certain seasons, alone.

Rooting further into the underground, I continued to hope that I would find rest where I was now landing.

I walked slowly into the darkening trees, encumbered by all of what I felt returning, and coming alive.

ᨕ

When the snow began to fall in geometric patterns, it was late January, in the season of wintering silence.

Singular flakes fell as elegant, transforming bearers of precipitation, and staring upward into the sky, no uniquely separable, ineffable contours could be seen.

I pressed my cold legs up the steep terrain as I trekked uphill from a descended path of forest to an open meadow, and toward the old dirt road that led back to my house. The cold air filled me within the cavity of my lungs, invigorating my spirit from the cagey and subdued restfulness of cabin fever.

My wrists were still sore from stacking a cord of wood in the barn the afternoon before as I tapped my winter boots on the frame of the mudroom in the back of the house with a bundle of firewood underneath my arm. I twisted the knob of the back door and turned back to see my footprints in the snow. A small movement caught my eye as a drop of snow fell from a branch, and the weight of a leaf lifted in the air.

Somewhere, the birds of winter remained—present, flittering, and obscured.

Inside, simmering chicken stock filled the air with the smell of vegetables and garlic as the old woodstove creaked and breathed warmth into the rooms inside. Everything now was nested and clean—the carpets replaced, walls painted, ducts and chimneys cleaned. The logs fell from my arm one by one as Lucy rubbed my leg, welcoming me back from my morning journey before meandering her way to the window. I stacked the wood along the brick wall behind the stove as burning logs crackled behind the stove door left slightly ajar.

The living room window slightly open let the winter air inside, and brisk cold whipped through the open crack with a subtle whisper. I slid the window shut and went into the kitchen to pour a bitter cup of steaming tea from the kettle, sweetening it with cream and a pinch of sugar, before making my way back to the living room, where Lucy stood perched on the back of my reading chair, pressing her front legs onto the cold glass to look outside the window. I stroked the magpie fur that ran softly across her back as she stared at the falling flakes from above.

And then, I fell tiredly into the corner of my couch, covering my legs with the comforting thick of a nearby blanket.

And I too stared out into the silence.

Flakes fell from an indiscernible sky. Unique and individual at first, some found their way together midair, becoming something wholly new, while all made their way to the ground—and for a time, all was untouched and without flaw.

Snow had been falling for days, and I breathed in the solitude.

I felt weighted in an earthy, invigorating place of newness. I remembered the changes in my foundation toward that grounding had been only a moment ago and knew better than to forget the way we are never so far from ourselves or the stories of our past. The contours of my own life's slight degrees of separation were marking their differences from where I used to be to where I now was, and as I stared into my tea, for a moment I saw the rivers of past and present diverge and then blend as they lapsed through time.

Outside, a winter bird echoed a lone song. I looked up from the steaming hot inside my hands, and the song was gone.

We are always in process with the many parts of ourselves, as what settles and becomes new lies beside all that remains unfinished.

The flicker of red-and-brown feathers caught my eye, disappeared for a moment, then sat perched along the fence, and I was encapsulated in the beauty of the falling.

When it was spring again, two years since I crossed innumerable waters to enter this door, thin-laced Swedish curtains blew gently in a returning breeze that passed through my windows. The translucent veils filled my home with delicate, softly whispering reminders—that life is always defined within and without the walls of ourselves.

Newly born lambs were wandering the pastures nearby, not far from their mother's milk, and as I walked across the road, one turned toward my presence, as I perched my foot on the wavering wood of a fence, and crossing my arms over the top, smiled, and reached out my hand.

I will spend a lifetime understanding the landscape within and around me, never fully reaching that desired destination. Maybe our true *home* isn't here at all, but in the meantime, my reflections of what it means to cultivate home inside will continue to ripple from within my own spirit out to where I touch yours. Perhaps somewhere in the spaces between where we all come together, we will together and alone become something more whole.

In the evening, I watched those who were dear walk home with bundles of lilac petals that once dripped from green trees and were now gently gripped within their swinging hands, after I'd cut the bloom down from the vine, smelling their sweet fragrance as they fell, and feeling the weight of those branches lighten toward the sky.

We weave and re-weave again through time and across great distances all parts of ourselves, and for a time, those stories settle together into a tapestry, like the sheet I now lie upon over the fresh cut grass outside my door. As budding lavender bends to reach me, and I lay my head upon the ground, and for a moment that I know will not last forever, I feel full held.

When I lean deep into a wooden chair that creaks at the end of the day, I see tall pieces of hay-like grass have woven themselves like straw through the fence, and a few of the stems rustle in the blowing wind. The sunlight is dipping behind flowering trees full and fat that rustle on the breeze—a dance completely their own.

Along the road, a dozen swallows together sing both in and out of harmony, and soon a few are circling and dashing as they fly in the broad sky above me, landing in their nest tucked beneath the shafts of my roof. I laugh and watch them for a moment, before returning my gaze from the heights of the sky to what lies on the ground before me.

The grass I cut before it grew too long smells sweet and green, and the barn behind the house begins to darken in the shade in the passing hours of the day.

A dragonfly buzzes by in a zigzag on the air.

And a honeybee cuddles seekingly into a flower.

Shadows of the shade of leaves dance over the page of my book as I read beside a tree, and I breathe, thinking we are meant to be more in the sound of the leaves and the birds than the bustled workings of the world. When I close my eyes for a still moment of rest, I fall into a filled and empty peace.

As I sit on my front steps in the morning hours, I sense what I am weaving together.

The shelves along the staircase are still broken; and the paint still chipping on the outside of the house.

Nothing is finished.

But as I stand, to go back inside the place I now call home, I pass through the threshold, and leave the door open to see what still might blow through.

In the night, in the quiet of my room, the moon shines through my window, down from a sleeping sky that casts small, moving glows beneath the dark. All around me, the house lies resting. Lucy cuddles beneath my arm, and I feel her body rising and falling, as she breathes.

I don't sense the darkness the way I did when I wandered in that other season before.

I find a greater restfulness from having sifted through so many sands and landing outwardly in a life that reflects my soul.

To continue may require more courage from me than I might sometimes believe I have, and through the vulnerable, delicate, resilient, and uncertain—I know just as well, the ways I am not always strong.

I know the ways that I am not always strong.

On the many paths I find inside myself—within this small country house, on a dead-end street that comes in and out on a path that is one and the same road—I will continue forward, even if I again shake and tremble in the dark.

As the wind stirs the leaves outside my open window, sweeping the subtle stillness of the night aside, a lone owl calls from somewhere on a branch not far beneath the sky. I remember the ineffable something that cannot be named or placed—

but in this dark, I do not feel fear, or doubt.

I fall into heavy slumber, and echoing remnants of you who I have touched speak into my dreams, and somehow through the passing of time, I know enough of myself is loved—because, and despite, of who I am.

Love will not always be reflected in what is within and around me—

but I will dip into its shimmering eternal remembrances
to remind myself of its truths just the same.

Outside, the world sleeps.

A great conjoining of wholeness between everything that is living, that you and I may never fully see or understand.

The settledness within is where I must return when the seas get rough, or when tides within, or between you and I, might try to drag what is together, apart.

The seas ebb and flow, carrying us all from once harbored shores to others, anew. But through some sacred grit, a determination to keep becoming, and perhaps a touch of patience, I have found I stay anchored enough through the seasonal tides that will always come, and eventually pass, and fade away.

For now, these farmlands are where I will lay my head as soft petals open to early life, amid a descent that reaches farther down and helps me discern through quiet sensing I hope will one day echo wisdom—when will be my time to go.

Perhaps if I stay rooted long enough, then moving forward again will no longer be the same as running away.

Every moment passes.

As life becomes so bountiful, memories of the past continue to profuse what has been planted within my soul.

Far beyond the confines of time
    is a music that still calls:
"Time is now fleeting,
the moments are passing
passing from you, and from me.
Shadows are gathering,
death night is coming.
Coming for you,
and for me.
Come home—
Come home…"

Ye who are weary, come home.

About the Author

Photo by Alexandria Kelly

Christina A. Kemp grew up in the Pacific Northwest. She has a Master of Arts in Counseling Psychology, and is a writer and teacher who has taught in the field of psychology. She has a small, private practice and teaches dance to children. *Across the Distance* is her first book. She lives on Bainbridge Island, Washington.